How You
Can
Be Healed

Fourteen Steps to Your Healing

Dr Michael h Yeager

Copyright © 2016 Dr Michael H Yeager
All rights reserved.
ISBN:1530562104
ISBN-13:9781530562107

DEDICATION

All of the Scriptures used in this book on **"How You Can Be Healed"** is from the original 1611 version of the King James Bible. I give thanks to God the Father , Jesus Christ and the Holy Ghost for the powerful impact the word has had upon my life. Without the word Quickened in my heart by the Holy Ghost I would've been lost and undone. To the Lord of Heaven and Earth I am eternally indebted for his great love and his mercy, his protections and his provisions, his divine guidance and overwhelming goodness, the Price He PAID for my Healing! To him be glory and praise for ever and ever: Amen .

CONTENTS

ACKNOWLEDGMENTS

*To our heavenly Father and His wonderful love.

*To our Lord, Savior and Master — Jesus Christ, Who saved us and set us free because of His great love for us.

*To the Holy Spirit, Who leads and guides us into the realm of truth and miraculous living every day.

*To all of those who had a part in helping me get this book ready for the publishers.

*To my Lovely Wife, and our precious children, Michael, Daniel, Steven, Stephanie, Catherine Yu, who is our precious daughter-in-law, and Naomi, who is now with the Lord.

Important Introduction

The HEALING'S I have seen, experienced, and share in this book are all true. They have happened personally to me, my family and others. These healings are recalled and shared to the best of my ability.

By no means do the following stories account for all the healings and miracles that we have seen, and experienced in my live. If we would recount every single answer to prayer, and every wonderful healing, miracle and blessing, there would be no end to this book!

What I am about to share with you in this book are simply some highlights of what we have experienced in the Lord. Some of these experiences will seem to be incredulous, however, they are true. This is not a testimony of how spiritual we are, but how wonderful and marvelous the Father, the Son, and the Holy Ghost are! I share these experiences to the best of my recollections and understanding. Not every conversation I share in these experiences are exactly word for word. I would love to name every person that was a part of these wonderful occurrences, but privacy laws do not allow this. If you are reading this book and you saw, experienced, or were a part of these events, please do not be offended because your names were not mentioned.

CHAPTER ONE

How You Can Be Healed!

The name of this Book could have been **"How You Can Be Healed & Delivered Without Me"**. I know this sounds strange, but the reason I make this statement is that many people have been emailing me, messaging me, even calling my church office trying to get help in the area of healing, but I am not able to get to every one! Many of you will never be able to attend the services I minister in. Many are telling me that they do not know of any place where they can go where the ministers are really strong in the **Promise of Divine healing**. So I have written this Book, hoping that what I am writing is going to help you get healed! Fourteen steps you can take to receive your Healing! Here is step number one!

#1 Enter into the Realm of Faith!

The very first principles, or step in receiving your healing is that you must get into the realm of faith. Jesus taught more on the subject of faith (in the four Gospels) than any other subject. This place, this dimension, this world that we call **FAITH**, is beyond the human equation, or understanding. This goes way beyond the intellect, your feelings, your emotions, and the circumstances of life. Isaiah chapter 55 he says:

*Isaiah 55:8 For my thoughts are not your thoughts, neither are your ways my ways, saith the Lord. 9 For as the heavens are higher than the earth, so are my ways higher than your ways, and my thoughts than your thoughts.

In order to get into this reality of **Faith**, it must be accomplished by way of the word of God. The Bible says that natural men did not dream up this book, **the Bible**, but spoke, and wrote as God moved upon them.

*2 Peter 1:21 For the prophecy came not in old time by the will of man: but holy men of God spake as they were moved by the Holy Ghost.

We can look at Hebrews chapter 11, where we see amazing miracles, signs, and wonders all accomplished by faith, by men and women just like you and I. In the New Testament, and in the Old Testament, all the way to the end of the Bible, people lived and moved by faith. The only way to get into this world, this realm, this place of **Faith,** were all things are possible, is by unwavering trust and confidence in God, and His Word. Everything that I will share with you in this book is to help bring you into this place called **Faith.** Without faith it is impossible to please God.

*Hebrews 11:6 But without faith it is impossible to please him: for he that cometh to God must believe that he is, and that he is a rewarder of them that diligently seek him.

Faith is like a diamond with many facets, and yet it is the same diamond!

Faith is spoken of in a very strong way (believe, trust,) over 800 times in the Bible. **Jesus** did more teaching on the subject of faith than anything other subject. I cannot over emphasize the importance of having faith in Christ to be **HEALED.** Before we can really go any further I need to explain what I mean when I say faith. As I read the word of God I discover there is *only one true* *faith*, that is faith in **CHRIST JESUS**! All other faiths and beliefs, no matter what you may call them, according to the word of God, they are not faith at all! It may be a belief system, a psychological philosophy, but it is not faith.

When Christ ascended up on high he gave gifts unto men. He gave some apostles, some prophets, some evangelist, pastors and teachers. Now these men and women need to be walking in the **Realm of Faith**. If they are not walking in faith, they cannot bring you into faith. IF they are not walking in obedience, they cannot bring you into a place of obedience. If they are not walking in deliverance, and freedom, they cannot bring you into that place.

Now, if we as ministers are not walking in **Healing**, how can we bring you into that realm of **Healing**? These fivefold ministry gifts that Christ gave should be, and need to be walking in this realm of faith. I'm not discrediting these men and women if they are not walking there, but it will be very difficult for these ministry gifts to help you receive what God has for you if they are not walking in it themselves. Basically we take people to the place where we are at.

The name of this book is **How You Can Be Healed** (and delivered without me). That means you can get healed on your own. You can get healed and delivered without having anyone pray for you. All the promises of divine healing revealed within God's word is available for you. Hebrew 11 gives to us a description of faith, and its manifestations. Let's look very briefly at Hebrews 11: 1to 3

Hebrews 11:1-3 <u>Now faith</u> is the <u>substance</u> of things hoped for, the <u>evidence</u> of things not seen. ² For by it the elders obtained a good report. ³ Through <u>faith</u> we understand that the worlds were framed by the word of God, so that things which are seen were not made of things which do appear.

So we can boldly declare that faith is a substance --- that gives evidence -- by which the worlds were framed by the word of God.

3

Only the Christian faith (faith in **CHRIST JESUS**) is what brought about, and continues to sustain creation, and all that exist. It is very important for us to understand that there is **only one faith**! This faith is the **only faith** that saves, heals, delivers, creates, pleases God, and makes all things possible!

Ephesians 4:4-6 There is one body, and one Spirit, even as ye are called in one hope of your calling; ⁵ one Lord, <u>one faith</u>, one baptism, ⁶ one God and Father of all, who is above all, and through all, and in you all.

Did you hear that? There is only **one true faith**, and that is faith in **CHRIST JESUS**! There is no other name under heaven given among men whereby we must be saved, healed, delivered, set free, and transformed! **TRUE FAITH** always takes dominion over the world, the flesh, and the devil! Faith in **Christ** always produces positive results, and brings victory in every situation. Many people are operating in presumption, natural reasoning, mental acknowledgment, truly thinking that they are operating in faith (In **Christ Jesus**) when the truth of the matter is --- **they are not!**

1 John 5:3-5 For this is the love of God, that we keep his commandments: and his commandments are not grievous. ⁴ For whatsoever is born of God overcometh the world: and this is the victory that overcometh the world, even our faith. ⁵ Who is he that overcometh the world, but he that believeth that Jesus is the Son of God?

Every human being when they were conceived within their mother's womb was invested with the divine seed of faith. It is extremely important that **we acknowledge this reality** in order that we do not allow our enemy (the devil) into deceiving us into believing that we have no faith. Not only were we created with faith, but we were created by faith, by **Christ Jesus, God the Father, and the Holy Ghost!**

John 1:3 *All things were made by him; and without him was not anything made that was made.*

**Let's take a look at two scriptures discovered in Genesis!
Genesis 1:26**

*And God said, Let us make man in our <u>image</u>, after our likeness:
and let them have dominion over the fish of the sea, and over the
fowl of the air, and over the cattle, and over all the earth, and
over every creeping thing that creepeth upon the earth. :27 So
God created man in his own <u>image</u>, in the image of God created
he him; male and female created he them.*

Did you notice that man was created in the image of God! How
does God operate and function? We could talk about the character
of God dealing with his love, mercy, forgiveness, long- suffering,
gentleness, kindness, meekness, holiness, faithfulness, joy,
goodness, and many other attributes, but all of these springs from
the fact that he operates in faith. There is a very interesting
Scripture that declares this found in the book of Timothy.

*2 Timothy 2:13 If we believe not, yet he abideth faithful: he
cannot deny himself.*   And in Romans it declares..........

*Romans 3:3 For what if some did not believe? Shall their
unbelief make the faith of God without effect?*

All of creation is sustained, maintained, and consists upon the
reality of God having faith in **Himself**. We were created and made
to walk in that realm of faith by trusting and having confidence,
total reliance, complete dependence upon nothing but God. The
only way the enemy could defeat man was by getting him out of
the arena of faith. He had to sow the seed of unbelief into the soil
of man's heart. Adam and his wife took the bait, thereby stepping
out of the realm of faith, into a nightmare of death, poverty, fear,
hate, lust, disobedience, sickness, and disease.
A Pandora's Box had been opened.

Christ Jesus came to shut that box, by bringing men back into
a position of absolute total faith, confidence, trust, obedience and

dependence upon God. Let's look in John 1:9 because within it is the evidence that at our conception God gave us faith.

John 1:9 That was the true Light, which lighteth <u>every man</u> that cometh into the world.

This light which lighteth up every man that comes into the world is the seed of faith, trust and confidence in God. **Jesus** boldly declared that in order to enter into the kingdom of heaven, we must have the faith of a child! Everything that **Jesus** ever spoke, was absolute truth. There was no exaggeration in anything he declared. Everything he spoke is absolute, complete, and total truth. We can and must base our life totally upon what he declared!

Matthew 18:3 And said, Verily I say unto you, Except ye be converted, and become as little children, ye shall not enter into the kingdom of heaven.

Mark 10:15 Verily I say unto you, Whosoever shall not receive the kingdom of God as a little child, he shall not enter therein.

Luke 18:17 Verily I say unto you, Whosoever shall not receive the kingdom of God as a little child shall in no wise enter therein.

Jesus was declaring unless you once again have the faith of a little child (this is true conversion) you will never be able to enter in! We could look at all the attributes of a little child, which I believe is a natural manifestation of true faith in **Christ**! If you will believe the Scripture I am about to share, It will clear up much confusion when it comes to those who have **not heard** the gospel. Please understand faith simply takes God at his word without any argument or doubting. *Romans 1:20-21 For the invisible things of him from the creation of the world are clearly seen, being understood by the things that are made, even his eternal power and Godhead; so that they are without excuse: [21] Because that, when they knew God, they glorified him not as God, neither were thankful; but became vain in their imaginations, and their foolish heart was darkened.*

Did you notice that it says that man is without excuse because at some time he understood? I know this sounds extremely strange, but it's true. Well how would a child understand? Part of this mystery can be answered by Hebrews 11:3

Hebrews 11:3 Through faith we understand that the worlds were framed by the word of God, so that things which are seen were not made of things which do appear.

When faith is alive and active, it literally understands, not with human reasoning, but from the inner depths of the heart. At the conception of every human being there was this invisible substance called faith. Now the day came when a person knowingly, and willingly goes against the faith that is in his heart, thereby entering into a condition of what God calls death. Death is when you no longer have a pure, and holy faith in God out of the sincerity of your heart. It is when you willingly, and knowingly break the laws of God.

Remember when Mary told Elizabeth her aunt that she was going to have a baby. That this baby was literally the son of God. What took place at that moment? It tells us that John within her womb, as an infant leaped for joy. What caused this excitement in the heart of the unborn child John? He was **full of faith**. He understood in his mother's womb that **Jesus** was the son of God, the Lamb of God, and that he had come into the Earth. This brought tremendous joy to his heart. This is another reason why he could be filled with the spirit from his mother's womb, because the Holy Ghost dwells in the atmosphere of faith.

Romans 7:9 For I was alive without the law once: but when the commandment came, sin revived, and I died.

Jesus Christ came to resurrect within the heart of every man complete and absolute faith, trust, confidence, dependence, reliance, and obedience to God the **Father**! Do not allow the enemy to tell you that you were born without faith. Faith is your natural habitat, dwelling place, just like the birds in the air, and the fish in the sea. Step back in to your rightful position.

It is important for us to understand that when we are born into this world that every part of our existence still needs to be developed. Whether it be our bones, muscles, organs, even our thinking and reasoning processes. **Even so it is with Faith**. Our faith must be developed, grow, become strong. This particular book is dealing with the subject of healing, but I have written other books dealing with the subject of faith. One particular book that I have written is dealing with how your faith can grow, mature and be developed by 28 ways. **How Faith Comes!** I would strongly encourage you to purchase this book at Amazon. This book is available for free, or only $.99 as a Kindle book, or e-book. Here is a little explanation of what this book covers.

How Faith Comes! [28 WAYS THAT FAITH COMES!]

For over 40 years of Ministry I probably have heard taught less than two biblical ways that faith comes. But in 2008 as I was in prayer early in the morning the spirit of God opened up my understanding, instantly downloading into me 28 major ways of **HOW FAITH COMES** within three minutes. I sat down at the dinner table absolutely flabbergasted, taking a pen and paper, and writing down what the Lord showed me. It took me days to write what I had seen in about three minutes. This revelation continues to flow to this day giving me deeper understandings on the important subject of faith in **Christ**! The Lord showed me supernaturally, and verified by Scriptures that there are approximately 28 ways that faith comes. This has been a progressive revelation. I am convinced that these are not the only ways that faith comes, but at this time it is the revelations that I have from God and his word.

How Faith Comes 28 Ways is not a new revelation, in the sense that it has always been there. Many of these 28 ways in which FAITH comes you will discover you have already been practicing, but now with a much clearer understanding you will be able to exercise yourself in these ways in a more persistent way in order to develop your FAITH in JESUS CHRIST!

Broken Foot Instantly Healed by the Gift of FAITH! (1996)

One day I had to climb our 250 foot AM radio tower in order to change the light bulb on the main beacon. However, in order to climb the tower, I had to first find the keys; which I never did. Since I could not find the keys to get the fence open, I did the next best thing—I simply climbed over the fence.

This idea turned out not to be such a wonderful idea after all! With all of my climbing gear hanging from my waist, I climbed the fence to the very top. At this point, my rope gear became entangled in the fencing. As I tried to get free, I lost my balance and fell backwards off the fence. Trying to break my fall, I got my right foot down underneath me. I hit the ground with my foot being turned on its side and I felt something snap in the ankle. I knew instantly I had a broken foot, my ankle.

Most normal people would have climbed back over the fence, go set up a doctor's appointment, have their foot x rayed, and then placed into a cast. But I am not a normal-thinking person, at least according to the standards of the modern day church. When I broke my foot, I followed my routine of confessing my stupidity to God, and asking Him to forgive me for my stupidity. Moreover, then I spoke to my foot and commanded it to be healed in the name of Jesus Christ of Nazareth. When I had finished speaking to my foot, commanding it to be healed, and then praising and thanking God for the healing, there seem to be no change what so ever in its condition.

The Scripture that came to my heart was where Jesus declared, "The kingdom of heaven suffereth violence, and the violent take it by force!" Based completely upon this scripture, I decided to climb the tower by faith, with a broken foot mind you. Please do not misunderstand, my foot hurt so bad I could hardly stand it. And yet, I had declared that I believed I was healed.

There were three men watching me as I took the Word of God by faith. I told them what I was about to do, and they looked at me like as if I had lost my mind. I began to climb the 250 foot tower, one painful step at a time. My foot hurt so bad that I was hyperventilating within just twenty to thirty feet up the tower. It literally felt like I was going to pass out from shock at any moment. Whenever I got to the point of fainting, I would connect my climbing ropes to the tower, stop and take a breather, crying out to Jesus to help me. It seemed to take me forever to get to the top.

Even so, I finally did reach the very top of the tower and replaced the light bulb that had gone out. Usually I can come down that tower within 10 minutes, because I would press my feet against the tower rods, and then slide down, just using my hands and arms to lower myself at a very fast pace. However, in this situation, my foot could not handle the pressure of being pushed up against the steel. Consequently, I had to work my way down very slowly. After I was down, I slowly climbed over the fence one more time. I hobbled my way over to my vehicle, and drove up to the church office. The men who had been watching this unfold, were right behind me.

I hobbled my way into the front office; which is directly across the street from the radio tower. I informed the personnel that I had broken my foot, showing them my black and blue, extremely swollen foot. It did not help that I had climbed with it! I told them that I was going home to rest. At the same time, however, I told them that I believed I was healed.

Going to my house, which is directly across from the main office of the church parking lot, I made my way slowly up the stairs to our bedroom. I found my wife in the bedroom putting away our clothes. Slowly and painfully I pulled the shoe and sock off of the broken foot. What a mess! It was fat, swollen, black and blue all over. I put a pillow down at the end of the bed, and carefully pulled myself up onto the bed. Lying on my back, I tenderly placed my broken, black and blue, swollen foot onto the pillow. No matter how I positioned it, the pain did not cease. I just laid there squirming, moaning and sighing.

As I was lying there trying to overcome the shock that kept hitting my body, I heard the audible voice of God. He said to me: "What are you doing in bed? "God really got my attention when I heard him with my natural ears. My wife would testify that she heard nothing. Immediately in my heart I said: Lord I'm just resting. Then He spoke to my heart with the still small voice very clearly, Do you always rest at this time of day? No, Lord, I replied.(It was about 3 o'clock in the afternoon)

He spoke to my heart again and said: I thought you said you were healed?

At that very moment the gift of faith exploded inside of me. I said, "Lord, I am healed! "Immediately, I pushed myself up off of the bed, grabbed my sock and shoe, and struggled to put them back on. What a tremendous struggle it was! My foot was so swollen that it did not want to go into the shoe. My wife was watching me as I fought to complete this task. You might wonder what my wife was doing this whole time as I was fighting this battle of faith. She was doing what she always does, just watching me and shaking her head. I finally got the shoe on my swollen, black and blue foot. I put my foot down on the floor and began to put my body weight upon it. When I did, I almost passed out. At that moment, a holy anger exploded on the inside of me. I declared out loud, "I am healed in the name of Jesus Christ of Nazareth!" With that declaration, I took my right (broken) foot, and slammed it down to the floor as hard as I possibly could.

When I did that, I felt the bones of my foot break even more. Like the Fourth of July, an explosion of blue, purple, red, and white, black exploded in my brain and I passed out. I came to lying on my bed. Afterward, my wife informed me that every time I passed out, it was for about ten to twenty seconds. The moment I came to, I jumped right back up out of bed. The gift of faith was working in me mightily. I got back up and followed the same process again, "In the name of Jesus Christ of Nazareth I am healed," and slammed my foot down once more as hard as I could! For a second time, I could feel the damage in my foot increasing. My mind was once again wrapped in an explosion of colors and pain as I blacked out.

When I regained consciousness, I immediately got up once again, repeating the same process. After the third time of this happening I came to with my wife leaning over the top of me. I remember my wife saying as she looked at me, "You're making me sick. I can't watch you do this." She promptly walked out of our bedroom, and went downstairs.

The fourth time I got up declaring, "In the name of Jesus Christ of Nazareth I am healed," and slammed my foot even harder! Once more, multiple colors of intense pain hit my brain. I passed out again! I got up the fifth time, angrier than ever. This was not a demonic or proud anger. This was a divine gift of violent I-will-not-take-no-for-an-answer type of faith. I slammed my foot down the fifth time, "In the name of Jesus Christ of Nazareth I am healed!" The minute my foot slammed into the floor, for the fifth time, the power of God hit my foot. I literally stood there under the quickening power of God, and watched my foot shrink and become normal. All of the pain was completely and totally gone. I pulled back my sock, and watched the black and blue in my foot disappear to normal flesh color. I was healed! Praise God, I was made whole! I went back to the office, giving glory to the Lord and showing the staff my healed foot.

CHAPTER TWO

#2 Be Extremely Serious!

The second step in your healing is that you must become very serious about your healing. You must even go beyond the word serious to the place of truly meaning business, or you could say: **get to the point of being desperate**. Yes, you must become desperate to be healed, desperate to be delivered, desperate to be made whole. **The Bible says the kingdom of heaven suffers violence, and the violent take it by force.** I want you to know that you **MUST** be serious, you have got to mean business. A major problem is that many Christians take the pathway of least resistance. It is so easy just to run off to the world and to get their help, and it is very easy just to run off to the doctors. It's easy to trust in the arm of the flesh. Please do not misunderstand me with the statements I am making. Truly I am not attacking people who use the world, but I'm simply stating the fact that in the midst of running to the world, instead of looking to God, we are literally tying the hands of God, and cutting our delves off from a Miracle. There are many scriptures that deal with not trusting God, and trusting man instead.

Jeremiah 17:5 Thus saith the Lord; Cursed be the man that trusteth in man, and maketh flesh his arm, and whose heart departeth from the Lord.

Psalm 118:8 It is better to trust in the Lord than to put confidence in man.9 It is better to trust in the Lord than to put confidence in princes.

Isaiah 2:22 Cease ye from man, whose breath is in his nostrils: for wherein is he to be accounted of

---

Psalm 146:3 Put not your trust in princes, nor in the son of man, in whom there is no help.4 His breath goeth forth, he returneth to his earth; in that very day his thoughts perish.

---

2 Chronicles 32:8 With him is an arm of flesh; but with us is the Lord our God to help us, and to fight our battles. And the people rested themselves upon the words of Hezekiah king of Judah.

Isaiah 31:1 Woe to them that go down to Egypt for help; and stay on horses, and trust in chariots, because they are many; and in horsemen, because they are very strong; but they look not unto the Holy One of Israel, neither seek the Lord!

God wants us to trust Him, God wants us to come to Him, God wants to help us, God wants us to believe him, but He is not going to make you. The **second step** you must take in you being healed is that you have to become serious, very serious, you could even say desperate when it comes to receiving your healing. **Pacifism** will open the door for the devil to kill you when it comes to your healing. There is no room for pacifism in this fight of faith, because we are not dealing with flesh and blood, but principalities, and powers, rulers of darkness, and spiritual wickedness in high places. The thief, the devil has come to steal, kill, and to destroy you.

Acts 10:38 How God anointed Jesus of Nazareth with the Holy Ghost and with power: who went about doing good, and healing all that were oppressed of the devil; for God was with him.

We see many illustrations throughout the Scriptures of people getting serious about healing, and not one of them did God disappoint! In the book of Revelation when Christ was speaking to the church, he said he was not happy with them because they were lukewarm. They were lackadaisical, lay back, take it easy pacifist. He literally said because they were neither cold, nor hot, but because they were lukewarm, he would vomit them out of his mouth. As long as you are lukewarm in your attitude towards your healing it will be very difficult for you to receive your miracle. I would strongly encourage you to read these three events that occurred in the Gospels. The first event was a woman with an issue of blood, who pressed her way through the masses to get healed. The second event is about blind Bartimaeus. Even with the disciples of Jesus telling him to be quiet, he would not shut up until he had received from Christ that which he was believing for. The third event is about a Phoenician woman whose daughter needed to be delivered from demons. In this particular situation it would even appear that Jesus spoke words that were very offensive. The woman did not allow this to discourage her, but pressed in until Jesus answer her prayers, and her daughter was delivered. This is so vitally important when it comes to us receiving our healing, which Christ has already purchased for us.

Matthew 9:20 And, behold, a woman, which was diseased with an issue of blood twelve years, came behind him, and touched the hem of his garment:21 For she said within herself, If I may but touch his garment, I shall be whole.22 But Jesus turned him about, and when he saw her, he said, Daughter, be of good comfort; thy faith hath made thee whole. And the woman was made whole from that hour.

Mark 10:46 And they came to Jericho: and as he went out of Jericho with his disciples and a great number of people, blind Bartimaeus, the son of Timaeus, sat by the highway side begging.47 And when he heard that it was Jesus of Nazareth, he began to cry out, and say, Jesus, thou son of David, have mercy on me. 48 And many charged him that he should hold his peace: but he cried the more a great deal, Thou son of David, have mercy on me. 49 And Jesus stood still, and commanded him to be called. And they call the blind man,

saying unto him, Be of good comfort, rise; he calleth thee. 50 And he, casting away his garment, rose, and came to Jesus. 51 And Jesus answered and said unto him, What wilt thou that I should do unto thee? The blind man said unto him, Lord, that I might receive my sight. 52 And Jesus said unto him, Go thy way; thy faith hath made thee whole. And immediately he received his sight, and followed Jesus in the way.

Matthew 15:21 Then Jesus went thence, and departed into the coasts of Tyre and Sidon.22 And, behold, a woman of Canaan came out of the same coasts, and cried unto him, saying, Have mercy on me, O Lord, thou son of David; my daughter is grievously vexed with a devil.23 But he answered her not a word. And his disciples came and besought him, saying, Send her away; for she crieth after us.24 But he answered and said, I am not sent but unto the lost sheep of the house of Israel.25 Then came she and worshipped him, saying, Lord, help me.26 But he answered and said, It is not meet to take the children's bread, and to cast it to dogs.27 And she said, Truth, Lord: yet the dogs eat of the crumbs which fall from their masters' table.28 Then Jesus answered and said unto her, O woman, great is thy faith: be it unto thee even as thou wilt. And her daughter was made whole from that very hour.

This is a mystery of active and living faith being manifested in a person's life. If you are really serious and desperate you will be a be a doer of taking a hold of God and not letting go. Even in the world success is only achieved by those who are truly and extremely serious about what they are involved in. It is God's will to deliver you, to heal you, to make you whole, but it will take a violent faith. I have run into many believers who have a twisted, perverted view when it comes to divine healing. They truly believe that it must not be God's will for them to be healed because their healing did not come easy. I hope you realize that the salvation which Christ has purchased for us was not easily accomplished, or cheaply bought. When Jesus said:

John 14:12 Verily, verily, I say unto you, He that believeth on

me, the works that I do shall he do also; and greater works than these shall he do; because I go unto my Father.

The works he was referring to was the aggressive, violent, and desperate acts of faith that he accomplished, with him even going all the way to the whipping post, the cross, and the grave. He had determined in his heart that he would obey the Father in that which he was asked to do until its ultimate conclusion.

Isaiah 50:7 For the Lord God will help me; therefore shall I not be confounded: therefore have I set my face like a flint, and I know that I shall not be ashamed.

I have received many, (actually most) of my healings in the last 40 years by aggressively taking a hold of God, and not letting go. You have to take the bull by the horns, put the ax to the grinding wheel, make the dust fly, if you're going to get your healing. I am amazed at what people allow the medical world to do to them in order that they might be made whole. If we would only turn all of this desperation, this overwhelming seriousness towards the Lord, I believe we would see many more miracles, an healings in our lives. God had given the children of Israel the land that flowed with milk and honey, but did you notice that they had to fight for it. Paul the apostle said he had fought a good fight, and that he had finished his course. There must be a faith in your heart that rises up and takes a hold of God's promises when it comes to divine healing.

For over 40 years I have aggressively, violently, and persistently taken a hold of my healing. I refuse to let the devil rob me of what Jesus so painfully purchased. It is mine, and the devil cannot have it. The thought has never even enter my mind to go see a doctor when physical sickness attacked my body. You see I already have a doctor, his name is Jesus Christ of Nazareth. He is the great physician, and he has already healed me with his stripes. Yes, there has been times when the manifestation of my healing seemed like it would never come, but I knew, that I knew, that I knew by his stripes I was healed. Strong faith never considers the circumstances.

Romans 4:18-20, Who against hope believed in hope, that he might become the father of many nations, according to that which was spoken, So shall thy seed be. And being not weak in faith, he considered not his own body now dead, when he was about an hundred years old, neither yet the deadness of Sarah's womb: He staggered not at the promise of God through unbelief; but was strong in faith, giving glory to God;

God Raised my son when dying from rabies!

When my son Daniel was 16 years old in 2000, he brought home a baby raccoon. He wanted to keep this raccoon as a pet. Immediately, people began to inform me that this was illegal. I further learned that in order to have a raccoon in Pennsylvania, one had to purchase one from someone who was licensed by the state to sell them. The reason for this was because of the high rate of rabies carried among them. But stubbornness rose up in my heart against what they were telling me, and I ignored sound logic.

You see, I had a raccoon when I was a child. Her mother had been killed on the highway and left behind a litter of her little ones. I had taken one of the little ones and bottle-fed it, naming her Candy. I have a lot of fond memories of this raccoon, so when my son wanted this raccoon, against better judgment and against the law of the land, I said okay. I did not realize that baby raccoons could have the rabies virus lying dormant in them for months before it would manifest. I knew in my heart that I was wrong to give him permission to keep this raccoon. But, like so many when we are out of the will of God, we justify ourselves. We stubbornly ignore the price that we will have to pay because of our rebellion and disobedience.

Daniel named his little raccoon Rascal. And he was a rascal because he was constantly getting into everything. A number of months went by and one night my son Daniel told me that he had a frightening dream. I should've known right then and there that we needed to get rid of this raccoon. He said in his dream, Rascal grew up and became big like a bear and then attacked and devoured him.

Some time went by and my son Daniel began to get sick, running a high fever. One morning, he came down telling me that something was majorly wrong with Rascal. He said that he was wobbling all over the place and was bumping into stuff. Immediately, the alarm bells went off. I asked him where his raccoon was. He informed me that Rascal was in his bedroom. Immediately I went upstairs to his room, opening his bedroom door. And their Rascal was acting extremely strange. He was bumping into everything and had spittle coming from his mouth.

Immediately, my heart was filled with great dread. I had grown up around wildlife and farm animals. I had run into animals with rabies before. No ifs, ands or buts, this raccoon had rabies. I immediately went to Danny asking him if the raccoon had bitten him or if he had gotten any of Rascal's saliva in his wounds? He showed me his hands where he had cuts on them, informing me that he had been letting rascal lick these wounds. He had even allowed rascal to lick his mouth.

Daniel did not look well and was running a high grade fever. He also informed me that he felt dizzy. I knew in my heart that we were in terrible trouble. I immediately called up the local forest ranger. They put me on the line with one of their personnel that had a lot of expertise in this area. When I informed him of what was going on, he asked me if I was aware of the fact that it was illegal to take in a wild raccoon. I told him I did know but that I had chosen to ignore the law.

He said that he would come immediately over to our house to examine this raccoon and if necessary to take it with him. I had placed Rascal in a cage making sure that I did not touch him. When the forest ranger arrived, I had the cage sitting in the driveway. He examined the raccoon without touching it. You could tell that he was quite concerned about the condition of this raccoon. He looked at me with deep regret informing me that in his opinion with 30 years wildlife service experience, this raccoon definitely had rabies. He asked me if there was anyone who had been in contact with this raccoon with any symptoms of sickness. I informed him that for the last couple days my son Daniel had not been feeling well. As a matter of fact, he was quite sick. When I told him the symptoms that Daniel was experiencing, it was quite obvious the ranger was shaken and quite upset.

He told me that anybody who had been in contact with this raccoon would have to receive shots. He went on to explain that from the description of what my son Daniel was going through and considering the length of his illness, it was too late for him! He literally told me that he felt from his experience that there was no hope for my son. He fully believed that my son would die from rabies. He loaded the raccoon up in the back of his truck, leaving me standing in my driveway weeping. He said that he would get back to me as soon as they had the test results and that I should get ready for state officials to descend upon myself, my family and our church.

I cannot express to you the hopelessness and despair that had struck my heart at that moment. Just earlier in the spring, our little girl Naomi had passed on to be with the Lord at 4 ½ years old. And now my second son Daniel was dying from rabies. Both of these situations could've been prevented.

Immediately, I gathered together my wife, my first son Michael, my third son Steven, and my daughter Stephanie. We all gathered around Daniel's bed and began to cry out to God. We wept, cried, and prayed crying out to God. I was repenting and asking God for mercy. Daniel, as he was lying on the bed running a high fever and almost delirious, informed me that he was barely able to hang on to consciousness. He knew in his heart, he said, that he was dying!

After everyone disbursed from his bed with great overwhelming sorrow, I went into our family room where we had a wood stove. I opened up the wood stove which still had a lot of cold ashes from the winter. Handful after handful of ashes I scooped out of the stove, pouring it over my head and saturating my body, with tears of repentance and sorrow running down my face. And then I lay in the ashes. The ashes got into my eyes, mouth and nose and into my lungs, making me quite sick. But I did not care, all that mattered was that God would have mercy on us and spare my son and all our loved ones from the rabies virus. As I lay on the floor in the ashes, crying out to God with all I had within me, one could hear the house was filled with weeping, crying and praying family members.

All night long I wept and prayed, (about 16 hours) asking God to please have mercy on my stupidity. To remove the rabies virus not only from my son, but from everyone else that had been in contact with this raccoon. I also asked God to remove the virus from Rascal as a sign that he had heard my prayers. I continued in this state of great agony and prayer until early in the morning when suddenly, the light of heaven shined upon my soul. Great peace that passes understanding overwhelmed me. I got up with victory in my heart.

I went upstairs to check on my son Daniel. When I walked into his bedroom, the presence of God was tangible. The fever had broken and he was resting peacefully. Our whole house was filled with the tangible presence of God. From that minute forward, he was completely healed. A couple of days later, I was contacted by the state informing me that, to their amazement, they could find nothing wrong with the raccoon.

God had supernaturally removed the rabies virus not only from my son and those in contact with Rascal, but from the raccoon itself. Thank God that the Lord's mercy endures forever!

Scriptures On Healing

Jeremiah 17:14 - Heal me, O LORD, and I shall be healed; save me, and I shall be saved: for thou [art] my praise.

1 Peter 2:24 - Who his own self bare our sins in his own body on the tree, that we, being dead to sins, should live unto righteousness: by whose stripes ye were healed.

Jeremiah 33:6 - Behold, I will bring it health and cure, and I will cure them, and will reveal unto them the abundance of peace and truth.

Isaiah 53:5 - But he [was] wounded for our transgressions, [he was] bruised for our iniquities: the chastisement of our peace [was] upon him; and with his stripes we are healed.

James 5:15 - And the prayer of faith shall save the sick, and the Lord shall raise him up; and if he have committed sins, they shall be forgiven him.:14 - Is any sick among you? let him call for the elders of the church; and let them pray over him, anointing him with oil in the name of the Lord:

3 John 1:2 - Beloved, I wish above all things that thou mayest prosper and be in health, even as thy soul prospereth.

Matthew 10:1 - And when he had called unto [him] his twelve disciples, he gave them power [against] unclean spirits, to cast them out, and to heal all manner of sickness and all manner of disease.

Matthew 10:8 - Heal the sick, cleanse the lepers, raise the dead, cast out devils: freely ye have received, freely give.

Deuteronomy 7:15 - And the LORD will take away from thee all sickness, and will put none of the evil diseases of Egypt, which thou knowest, upon thee; but will lay them upon all [them] that hate thee.

CHAPTER THREE

#3 Never Exalt Afflictions!

The third step in your healing is that you **must never, never, ever** exalt the devil, your problems, the negative circumstances, the symptoms in your body, or your bad situation. **What do I mean by this statement?** I hear many Christians exalting their problems, and yet I have personally known believers that had major problems, but never talked about them, never made a big deal out of them, never even told people what they were going through.

One time when Smith Wigglesworth (who was an amazing man of Faith) had a real serious financial situation, he went to pray for a wealthy man. When he prayed for this wealthy man, the man was gloriously healed, and delivered right then and there! The wealthy man told Smith Wigglesworth that he wanted to bless him, asking if there was anything he could do to help him? He told the wealthy man: No brother, but thanked him any ways for the offer. Smith was literally looking to God to take care of a desperate financial need. By the way God did do an amazing miracle to meet this financial need.

On another occasion Smith Wigglesworth ended up with a terrible affliction of gallstones. When he was informed by a specialist that the only way of deliverance from these gallstones was by an operation, Smith Wigglesworth responded with:

"God Shall Operate"

His son-in-law, James Salter, said that during the whole three years of this trial, Smith never stopped preaching, never complained, or told anyone. Even though Smith Wigglesworth was in great pain, and bled a great deal, he continued to minister to the sick, even with blood running down his legs, filling his socks and shoes, as he laid hands on the sick. He did end up spend many days in bed in great pain, but would get up in order to make it to the meetings where he was to minister. This test supposedly went on day, after day, after another day, and night, after night.

It is reported that the meetings he conducted during this time were powerful, with many attesting to the wonderful miracles of God's healing power. When deliverance finally manifested in Smith Wigglesworth body, which was almost instantaneous, with all of the gallstones, 20 or more coming out. Smith Wigglesworth was made completely and perfectly whole. Smith put those stones in a small tin can and on occasions he would show the stones to different people as he told them of Gods faithfulness. Some of these stones were quite large: others were jagged and needle shaped. All of the stones not only caused tremendous pain, but penetrated his innards in such a way that it caused constant hemorrhaging. Smith was a man who understood what it meant to have faith that worked by patients. He had an unshakable faith that caused him to agree with God, and to disagree with the circumstances no matter the pain, or problem.

Whenever we exalt the sickness, the afflictions or the problems of our lives, we are operating in a spirit of unbelief. I am not saying that we cannot share privately with people of faith what we are going through in order that they can agree and believe with us. In over 40 years of walking with Christ, personally I have shared very little with people what I was being confronted with. I knew that most people were not truly going to be believing with me, but would simply tell others what I was going through. I would like to share with you a number of powerful examples of this in the four Gospels, in the ministry of Jesus. The first one we need to look at is with the father who had a demon possessed son.

Mark 9:17 And one of the multitude answered and said, Master, I have brought unto thee my son, which hath a dumb spirit; 18 And wheresoever he taketh him, he teareth him: and

he foameth, and gnasheth with his teeth, and pineth away: and I spake to thy disciples that they should cast him out; and they could not.

19 He answereth him, and saith, O faithless generation, how long shall I be with you? how long shall I suffer you? bring him unto me. 20 And they brought him unto him: and when he saw him, straightway the spirit tare him; and he fell on the ground, and wallowed foaming. 21 And he asked his father, How long is it ago since this came unto him? And he said, Of a child. 22 And ofttimes it hath cast him into the fire, and into the waters, to destroy him: but if thou canst do anything, have compassion on us, and help us. 23 Jesus said unto him, If thou canst believe, all things are possible to him that believeth. 24 And straightway the father of the child cried out, and said with tears, Lord, I believe; help thou mine unbelief. 25 When Jesus saw that the people came running together, he rebuked the foul spirit, saying unto him, Thou dumb and deaf spirit, I charge thee, come out of him, and enter no more into him. 26 And the spirit cried, and rent him sore, and came out of him: and he was as one dead; insomuch that many said, He is dead. 27 But Jesus took him by the hand, and lifted him up; and he arose.

In this particular incident I want you to notice how the father was more than willing to brag about the demonic afflictions that were upon his son. Jesus **never asked people what was wrong with them**, but would ask them what it was that they wanted. In most of these situations it was obvious what the people needed, but he would ask them what it was they wanted. In **Mark 11: 24** Jesus said: **whatsoever things you desire, when you pray, believe that you receive, and you shall have.** Jesus was always directing the needy to ask for what they needed, and **not to meditate upon the problem**.

On many occasions when Jesus was surrounded by people who were boasting on the devil, he would direct the needy away from them. We have the one illustration of this when the couple's daughter died! Let's take a moment to look at this particular Scripture.

Matthew 9:18 While he spake these things unto them, behold, there came a certain ruler, and worshipped him, saying, My daughter is even now dead: but come and lay thy hand upon her, and she shall live.19 And Jesus arose, and followed him, and so did his disciples....... 23 And when Jesus came into the ruler's house, and saw the minstrels and the people making a noise,24 He said unto them, Give place: for the maid is not dead, but sleepeth. And they laughed him to scorn.25 *But when the people were put forth,* he went in, and took her by the hand, and the maid arose.

Understand that none of us have arrived, and none of us are walking in 100% faith all the time. Sometimes I get out of the will of God, I panic, I look at the circumstances, I look at the problem. As I share these truths with you, I am not claiming that I have arrived. I am simply coming from the place in which I have had many experience, many wonderful results by simply following the principles (not a formula) of the word of God. We must never boast, never brag, never exalt the devil, and never ever exalt the circumstance that is contrary to the word of God. I can give you a lot of examples found in the bible when men and women contradicted Gods word, and exalted the problem, and it never ended well for them.

In Numbers 13 we discover a powerful illustration of this when the spies went into the land of promise that God had proclaimed flowed with milk and honey. When the 12 spies returned they acknowledged that what God said was true.

Numbers 13:27 And they told him, and said, We came unto the land whither thou sentest us, and surely it floweth with milk and honey; and this is the fruit of it.

Now, it is wonderful that they acknowledged that what God said is true, yet in their next words they demean the promise, and basically called God a liar, and that his promise of protecting and providing for them false. They exalted their enemies above God.

Numbers 13:28 Nevertheless the people be strong that dwell in the land, and the cities are walled, and very great: and moreover we saw the children of Anak there.29 The Amalekites dwell in the land of the south: and the Hittites, and the Jebusites, and the Amorites, dwell in the mountains: and the Canaanites dwell by the sea, and by the coast of Jordan.

This information that they began to spew forth was nothing new. God had already informed them about the enemy, with all of their tribal names, and at the same time he told them that their enemies would be bread for them to eat. Joshua and Caleb spoke up in the mist of their declaration, and declared that God was more than able if they would simply look to him, they would be able to overcome. If you read the context of this whole story you will sadly discover that they rose up against these two men of faith, against God, against Moses, and in a violent manner. They said that they would rather have stayed in Egypt, or died in the wilderness then go back into Canaan to overcome the enemy. God granted their wish by allowing the first generation out of Egypt to die in the desert.

I run into believers all the time, Christians, not sinners that have made devils, demons, the problems they are dealing with, sicknesses and diseases in their bodies, in their minds bigger than God. Now how can it be that the God who upholds all things with the power of his word is not able to overcome the problems of our life? From Genesis all the way to the end of the book of Revelation God reveals himself as more than enough in every situation. Every trial, every affliction, every test simply reveals how big you have made God in your life.

The question we all need to ask ourselves is: **How Big Is Our God?** It reminds me of the biblical story of David and Goliath. The Israel Army was confronted by the Philistines, who had a champion by the name of Goliath. Goliath had for 40 days challenged anybody to face him, but there were none in Israel's army that had enough faith in God to face him.

1 Samuel 17:4 And there went out a champion out of the camp of the Philistines, named Goliath, of Gath, whose height was six cubits and a span......10 And the Philistine said, I defy the armies of Israel this day; give me a man, that we may fight together.11 When Saul and all Israel heard those words of the Philistine, they were dismayed, and greatly afraid........16 And the Philistine drew near morning and evening, and presented himself forty days........

Here comes along a Shepherd boy by the name of David that says: who is this uncircumcised Philistine that should defy the armies of the living God? Now you have a whole army of men exalting their enemy, Goliath by name, and you have one young shepherd boy by the name of David saying: this man is nothing compared to my God. It might have sounded like David was just full of pride, but in reality it was faith speaking, because not only did he declare that Goliath was nobody, and nothing, but that he himself would be willing to face this man. I have met many believers who talk a big talk, but have little corresponding action.

Faith when it is in operation will never exalt, brag, or magnify that which is against the will of God. I hear believers all the time exalting their problems, their sicknesses, their afflictions, and their symptoms. When you are truly operating in faith you will only, and always exalt God, and his word. This is a tremendous way that I have discovered to find out **if I'm truly operating in faith.** My mouth gives me a way all the time, it reveals to myself where I am at. There is a tremendous Scripture given to us in the book of James pertaining to this reality.

James 1:22 But be ye doers of the word, and not hearers only, deceiving your own selves.23 For if any be a hearer of the word, and not a doer, he is like unto a man beholding his natural face in a glass:24 For he beholdeth himself, and goeth his way, and straightway forgetteth what manner of man he was.25 But whoso looketh into the perfect law of liberty, and

continueth therein, he being not a forgetful hearer, but a doer of the work, this man shall be blessed in his deed.

I could give you many examples of this in my own personal life, and the lives of others I have known. I remember one time we had a lady in our church. Her and her husband were quite wealth, and influential in our community. She was having some problems in her hands, so she went to the doctors to find out what was wrong. She came back from the doctors and she was crying, weeping, and she was all upset. I asked her what was wrong? She told me that the doctor said I might have: and she named a disease. She then informed me the doctor also said that it could possibly be another such and such disease. By the time he was done talking to her, he had mentioned five different afflictions, or diseases it could possibly be.

This Dr. had successfully filled this godly woman, this believer with fear and unbelief. The enemy loves to turn a molehill into a mountain, which we ignorantly and innocently begin to confess over our lives. Now even if it is truly a mountain God tells us that we can speak to the mountain and cast it into the sea. Never allow the devil to get you to exalt the sickness, disease, or afflictions in your body. For over 40 years I have purposely strived to never exalt the problem I'm experiencing, even if I'm not operating in faith. There is a Scripture in Ephesians that encourages us never to speak that which is contrary to God's word.

Ephesians 4:29 Let no corrupt communication proceed out of your mouth, but that which is good to the use of edifying, that it may minister grace unto the hearers.

There is another set of scriptures discovered in Philippians 4 that also encourages us along the same line.

Philippians 4:8 Finally, brethren, whatsoever things are true, whatsoever things are honest, whatsoever things are just, whatsoever things are pure, whatsoever things are lovely,

whatsoever things are of good report; if there be any virtue, and if there be any praise, think on these things.

We are living in a time when many believer's faith is so weak that they spend all of their time exalting their problems, exalting afflictions, exalting the infirmities in their body. The purpose of writing this book is not to demean people, but to help them come to the place of strong faith in Christ Jesus, to where they can be healed and made whole without even having people pray for them. We need to realize that the devil loves it when we are speaking death over ourselves. Negative words will draw demonic powers right to us. I remember as a young boy sitting around a campfire late at night and somebody would be sharing a terrible, dreadful, frightening story. In every one of these situations my heart began to be filled with great fear and dread, because unknown to us that as we were exalting demonic activities, it brought to us demonic powers. The opposite is also true when we begin to exalt Christ, God, and his word. As we begin to exalt the truth, the truth will draw God's divine presence to us, his power, his angelic beings, because Angels hearken to the voice of God's word!

Psalm 103:20 Bless the Lord, ye his angels, that excel in strength, that do his commandments, hearkening unto the voice of his word.

Psalm 81:13 Oh that my people had hearkened unto me, and Israel had walked in my ways!14 I should soon have subdued their enemies, and turned my hand against their adversaries.

James 4:8 Draw nigh to God, and he will draw nigh to you. Cleanse your hands, ye sinners; and purify your hearts, ye double minded.

Now please take heed to this spiritual truth, and whether you accept it, or not, this is absolute truth. In this world flowers will drawl to themselves honeybees, even as manure always draws flies. The word of God spoken out of your mouth, from your heart will always bring God's angels, God's presence, and God's power! Jesus said to the devil: **"It Is Written"** three times, in which immediately angelic beings appeared to minister to him.

Matthew 4:11 Then the devil leaveth him, and, behold, angels came and ministered unto him.

Angel appeared and strengthened him when he was in a the garden of Gethsemane praying that the heavenly Father's will would be accomplished in his life, instead of his own.

Luke 22:43 And there appeared an angel unto him from heaven, strengthening him.

Even as angelic beings hearken to the voice of God as you speak the word, so do demons respond when you exalt the devil, when you exalt sickness, when you exalt diseases. People hear the word **cancer**, and it fills their heart with absolute fear. The Scriptures boldly declare that fear has torment, and that it is not of God. *God has not given us a spirit of fear, but of power, love, and a sound mind*. On three different occasions I had the symptoms of cancer in my body. There were times when I had extremely painful tumors. On another occasion I had what appeared to be prostate cancer. One of my longest battles was when all indications declared that I had colon cancer. Let me share that experience, hoping it will give you spiritual insight in how we fight this battle of faith against all of the lies of the devil.

I Overcame Colon Cancer without doctors!

I began to experience some very disturbing symptoms in my body. I will not go into all the details but there were approximately nine different physical symptoms. One of the symptoms was almost every time when I had a bowel movement, it looked as if all my innards were coming out. During this 3-month period of time, I was so sick sometimes that I thought that I was going to die at any moment. My normal course of action is that the minute my body begins to manifest any kind of sickness or disease; I immediately command it to go in the Name of Jesus Christ of Nazareth!

Even though I was boldly speaking Gods Word these symptoms simply refuse to leave. I made a list of everything that was happening in my body, and then I looked these symptoms up on the internet. Every one of them pointed to colon cancer. I had gone through a similar fight of faith a number of years previously, with what seemed to be prostate cancer. Once again, I took hold of the Word of God. I boldly declared to the devil, myself and the spiritual world that I would live and not die. I cried out to Jesus for His mercy, and His grace in the midst of this fight of faith. This fight was almost overwhelming and excruciating at times!

For these three months I continued with this fight. I spoke to the symptoms commanding them to go. I kept praising, thanking and worshiping God that I was healed; no ifs, ands or buts. I declared boldly that the devil is a liar. For three months every day, all day at times, declaring what God said about me. I did not invite anybody else to stand with me in this fight of faith. Most people, if they would have known what I was going through, would have pronounced me dead, and gone. Believe it or not there are actually people who call themselves Christians who would've rejoiced in my death. Yes, they would've been telling people to pray, but there would have been more negative comments than the reality of God's Word. **By His stripes we were healed**! If I were healed, then I was healed, if I was healed than I am healed, and if I am healed, then I is healed!

For three long months I stood and fought by faith. Many nights and days walking the floor of our church sanctuary praising God that I was healed, resisting the spirit of fear. One day I woke up, and low and behold all of the symptoms had disappeared, praise God, and they have never come back. Thank you Jesus!!!

CHAPTER FOUR

#4 Exalt Christ in Your Heart!

Christ was the perfect will of the heavenly Father, manifested and revealed to us in his earthly ministry. We must now learn to exalt Jesus Christ above all and over all the afflictions in our bodies in order to be healed. Jesus has all authority and power in Heaven and in Earth!

Matthew 28:18 And Jesus came and spake unto them, saying, All power is given unto me in heaven and in earth.

Colossians 2:15 And having spoiled principalities and powers, he made a shew of them openly, triumphing over them in it.

For this particular chapter I will be using **Hebrews chapter 1**, and the gospel of **John chapter 1**. These two chapters will help build an amazing foundation for your healing, and spiritual discernment, when it comes to receiving your healing in every situation. If you will embrace what is revealed in these two chapters, your ability to receive healing from God will be greatly increased. Let us now take a look at Hebrews chapter 1.

Hebrews 1:1 God, who at sundry times and in divers manners spake in time past unto the fathers by the prophets, 2 hath in these last days spoken unto us by his Son, whom he hath appointed heir of all things, by whom also he made the worlds; 3 who being the brightness of his glory, and the express image of his person, and upholding all things by the word of his power, when he had by himself purged our sins, sat down on the right hand of the Majesty on high;

In Hebrews 1 it is revealed that God had spoken to the fathers by the prophets, but has now spoken to us by his son Jesus Christ. According to **Ephesians 2:20 the kingdom of God is built upon the apostles and prophets, Jesus Christ himself being the chief cornerstone.** Please notice that in times past God spoke specifically by the prophets to the father's, now we have a surer word of prophecy, a deeper revelation, a more precise understanding of the perfect will of our heavenly Father.

Why? Because he's going to speak to us in a very clear and dramatic way. If we will believe the words, the life, and the example of Jesus Christ, it will radically transform our lives forever. Remember all the words and deeds that had been spoken and revealed up to the time of Christ was to prepare us for the coming of Christ. The life of Jesus is the perfect will of God manifested in human flesh. This is the mystery which had been hidden before the foundation of the world.

Notice Hebrews 1: in verse 2 *hath in these last days spoken unto us by his Son!* The foundation of my understanding of the will of God, the purposes of God, the plan of God, the mission of God, the mysteries of God, cannot be discovered in any greater revelation than the person of Jesus Christ! **There is no greater revelation of God's perfect divine will or his voice then that which we discover in Jesus Christ.** I cannot emphasize this enough!

If you do not understand that God has revealed himself to us very precisely through his son Jesus Christ, you will end up being mixed up, confused, and led astray. Learning the will of God very precisely is only found in Jesus Christ, whom he has appointed heir of all things, by whom also he made the worlds. Notice Hebrews chapter 1:3 boldly declares that Jesus Christ is the brightness of the Father's glory, the manifestation of the Fathers presence, and the express image of His personality. Jesus is like a mirror reflecting the perfect image of the heavenly Father to all of humanity. Jesus declared:

John 14:9 Jesus saith unto him, have I been so long time with

you, and yet hast thou not known me, Philip? He that hath seen me hath seen the Father; and how sayest thou then, Shew us the Father? 10 Believest thou not that I am in the Father, and the Father in me? The words that I speak unto you I speak not of myself: but the Father that dwelleth in me, he doeth the works.

Jesus Christ is the absolute perfect will of the Father revealed to you and me, especially when it comes to healing. The deepest revelation of the Father is only discovered in Jesus Christ! Paul the apostle commands us to have the mind of Christ.

Philippians 2:5 Let this mind be in you, which was also in Christ Jesus: 6 who, being in the form of God, thought it not robbery to be equal with God: 7 but made himself of no reputation, and took upon him the form of a servant, and was made in the likeness of men: 8 and being found in fashion as a man, he humbled himself, and became obedient unto death, even the death of the cross.

When we look at Jesus and hear His words, see his works, it is the Father that we are experiencing! The apostle John boldly declares this in John 1.

John 1:1 In the beginning was the Word, and the Word was with God, and the Word was God. 2 The same was in the beginning with God. 3 All things were made by him; and without him was not anything made that was made.

All things were made by the word. What word is it speaking about in these scriptures? Is it talking about the written word or Christ the word? It is obvious that it is talking about the person of Christ Jesus, Emmanuel God with us!

John 1:14 And the Word was made flesh, and dwelt among us, (and we beheld his glory, the glory as of the only begotten of the Father,) full of grace and truth.

The reality is that we have to know the person of Christ discovered in the four Gospels in order for us to rightly discern the word of God. What do I mean by this statement? When I gave my heart to Jesus Christ on February 18, 1975, at about 3 PM in the afternoon, all I had available was a little military green Bible. At the moment Christ came into my heart I picked up that little Bible, and began to devour it. Matthew, Mark, Luke, and John, the 4 Gospels of Jesus Christ became my favorite books. I just could not get enough of the wonderful reality of Jesus. As I read these 4 Gospels I walked with Christ every step of the way. From his birth, through his childhood, his baptism by John when he was 30 years old. When he was baptized by the Holy Ghost, and he was led of the Spirit into the wilderness, tempted of the enemy and overcame him by boldly declaring **"It is written"**.

I spent my first three years as a believer eating and drinking nothing but Jesus from the four Gospels. Yes, I did read the epistles, and they were wonderful, but nothing captured and captivated my heart as much as the life, the words, and the ministry of Jesus Christ. I wept as I read of his sufferings, his crucifixion and his death. I wept when I saw that the Heavenly Father had to turn his face away from his own Son for our salvation. I shouted at the triumphant conquest and victory that Jesus had over every satanic power.

Jesus Christ is the perfect reflection of the Heavenly Father. There is no more perfect revelation of the will of the Father than Jesus Christ. Actually I am extremely happy that I was not influenced by the modern day church for the first three years of my salvation. When I eventually came to the lower 48, after living and ministering in Alaska, I was shocked and surprised at what most Christians believed. I did not realize that there was such a large variety of different interpretations of the Scriptures in the church. Many of God's people are extremely confused, sick, and defeated because of a lack of understanding the will of the Father revealed to us in the life, the ministry, the words of Jesus Christ. Many ministers declare insane false doctrines that are so contrary to what I discovered in Christ, it is hard for me to believe that people can even believe what these men are teaching is truth. To truly know the will of God, all you have to do is look at Jesus Christ: His words, deeds, actions and reactions; His lifestyle and his attitude, mannerism, wonderful character, and the fruit of his life. I can truly say that since I have been born again I have only had one person who I truly want to be like: **His name is Jesus Christ.**

If the body of Christ would simply go back to the four Gospels, and walk with Jesus every step of the way, from his birth to his resurrection, to his ascension, much of the confusion would be gone when comes to the will of God. I believe the reason why so many believers are being deceived by false doctrines and philosophies, why they are not receiving their healing is because they really do not know, or understand Jesus Christ.

Hebrews 13:8, "Jesus Christ the same yesterday, and today, and forever."

In the old covenant God says **"I am the Lord, and I change not"**. Without truly seeing the Father by the words of Jesus Christ, and by the life of Jesus Christ you can easily be led astray by crafty men misusing Scriptures. You have to see Jesus to understand not just the Old Testament but also the epistles of the New Testament. Jesus is the voice of God, the absolute perfect will of the Father, the manifestation of God in the earth.

I have actually heard ministers use the Bible to contradict the teachings of Jesus Christ. The reason why false doctrines have been able to take root in the church is because people have not really looked and listened to Jesus in the four Gospels. If in your mind and heart you will exalt Christ, and his teaching above all else, it will be very difficult for the enemy to lead you astray with false teachings and doctrines. Here is an example when it comes to the will of God pertaining to my own personal healings.

Why God heals me Every Time. 1975

While reading my Bible as a brand new believer, (1975) I discovered that Jesus Christ went about healing **ALL** who were sick and oppressed of the devil. I began to search the Scriptures on this particular subject, and as I studied I discovered many Scriptures that support this:

Surely he hath borne our griefs, and carried our sorrows: yet we did esteem him stricken, smitten of God, and afflicted. But he was wounded for our transgressions, he was bruised for our iniquities: the chastisement of our peace was upon him; and with his stripes we are healed (Isaiah 53:4-5).

Who his own self bare our sins in his own body on the tree, that we, being dead to sins, should live unto righteousness: by whose stripes ye were healed.1 Peter 2:24

When the even was come, they brought unto him many that were possessed with devils: and he cast out the spirits with his word, and healed all that were sick: That it might be fulfilled which was spoken by Esaias the prophet, saying, Himself took our infirmities, and bare our sicknesses. Matthew 8:16-17

As I read and meditated upon these Scriptures, something wonderful happened within my heart. Great, overwhelming sorrow took a hold of me as I saw the pain and the agony that Jesus went through for my healing. In my heart and in my mind I saw that Jesus had taken my sicknesses and my diseases. I then experienced a great love for the son of God, and recognize the price he paid for my healing. And then it happened! It was like an open vision in which I saw my precious **Lord and Savior** tied to the whipping post. I saw the Roman soldiers striking the back of Jesus with the cat of nine tails. In this vision I saw the flesh and the blood of my precious Savior sprinkling everything within a 10-foot radius, with each terrible strike of the soldier's whip causing his blood to splatter. As I saw this open vision, I wept because I knew it was for me this was done. To this day, even as I retell this story great love and sorrow fills my heart, yet I have great joy because I know that by the **stripes of Jesus I am healed**.

In this moment of this vision something exploded within my heart, an amazing faith possessed me with the knowledge that I no longer have to be sick. In the name of Jesus for over 40 years I have refused to allow what my precious Lord went through to be for nothing. I have refused to allow sickness and disease to dwell in my body, which is the temple of the Holy Ghost.

Jesus has taken my sicknesses and my diseases. No if, ans, or butts, no matter what it looks like or how I feel, I know within my heart Jesus Christ has set me free from sicknesses and diseases. At the moment of this revelation great anger, yes great anger, rose up in my heart against the enemy of my Lord. The demonic world has no right to afflict me or any other believer, because Jesus took our sicknesses and bore our diseases.

Now I had been born with terrible physical infirmities, but now I found myself speaking out loud with authority to my ears, commanding them to be open and to be normal in the name of Jesus Christ of Nazareth. Then I spoke to my lungs, and commanded them to be healed in the name of Jesus Christ of Nazareth. Next I commanded my sinuses to be delivered, so I could smell normal scents in the name of Jesus Christ of Nazareth.

The minute I spoke the Word of God to my physical man, my ears popped completely open. Up to this moment I had a significant hearing loss, but now as I was listening to Christian music playing softly (at least I thought it was) the music became so loud that I had to turn it down. My lungs were clear, and I haven't experienced any lung congestion since in 40 years. I used to be so allergic to dust that my mother had to work extra hard to keep our house dust-free. I would literally end up in an oxygen tent in the hospital. From that moment to now dust, allergies, mold, or any such thing have never come back to torment me or cause me problems. Instantly my sense of smell returned! I had broken my nose about four times due to fights, accidents, and rough activities. I could barely smell anything.

Suddenly, I could smell a terrible odor. I tried to find out where it was coming from and then I looked at my feet and wondered if it could be them. I put my foot on a night stand and bent over toward it. I took a big sniff and nearly fell over. Man, did my feet stink! I went straight over to the bathroom and washed them in the sink.

This portion is worth repeating. For Over 40 years I have aggressively, violently, persistently, taken a hold of my healing. I refuse to let the devil rob me of what Jesus so painfully purchased. It is mine, and the devil cannot have it. The thought does not even enter my mind to go see a doctor when physical sickness attack my body, for I already have a doctor, his name is **Jesus Christ** of Nazareth. He is the great physician, and he has already healed me with his stripes. Yes, there has been times when the manifestation of my healing seemed like it would never come, there has been many times when it looked like in the natural I was going to die, but I knew, that I knew, that I knew that by the stripes of Jesus I am healed. Jesus Christ is the final authority in my life when it comes to the divine will of the Father. His life, his word is the absolute voice of God pertaining to every situation. Without this revelation and foundation, the enemy will be able to easily lead you astray, and destroy you.

The very 1st thing we must do to build a solid foundation for our lives is to let go of all our traditions, philosophies, doctrines, and experiences that contradict what is revealed to us through Jesus Christ. We must go back to Matthew, Mark, Luke and John rediscovering who Jesus Christ really is. Whatever Jesus said and did is what we agree with wholeheartedly. Any voice or teaching that contradicts Christ, and his redemptive work I immediately reject.

John 10:3 To him the porter openeth; and the sheep hear his voice: and he calleth his own sheep by name, and leadeth them out.

John 10:27 My sheep hear my voice, and I know them, and they follow me:

John 10:4 And when he putteth forth his own sheep, he goeth before them, and the sheep follow him: for they know his voice.

Rev 3:20 Behold, I stand at the door, and knock: if any man hear my voice, and open the door, I will come in to him, and will sup with him, and he with me.

Prov 8:20 I lead in the way of righteousness, in the midst of the paths of judgment:21 That I may cause those that love me to inherit substance; and I will fill their treasures.

Isaiah 42:16 And I will bring the blind by a way that they knew not; I will lead them in paths that they have not known: I will make darkness light before them, and crooked things straight. These things will I do unto them, and not forsake them.

We must come to the place where Jesus is bigger than anything we are facing, anything afflicting us, anything that is out to destroy us! Once you kill the lion, then comes the bear, and from the bear comes Goliath! As your faith is growing you're going to have bigger obstacles, and opportunities that will confront you, this is how it works. It is just like in the world when you climb into the boxing arena, and you take on a fighter that you have never fought before. You must give it your all as you fight against this new adversary before you move up the ladder to the next one. You are not going to face the heavyweight champion of the world if you do not first work your way up through all of those lower adversaries. We have an adversary called the devil who will try to afflict us with sickness and disease, and we must overcome him. Our enemy the devil might hit us with a headache, it might be a toothache, it might be a backache, or even a broken back. Demonic spirits might hit us with lumps in our body, or a heart condition. All of these afflictions which I have just mentioned, I have personally experienced, and I have had to fight my way through them. The Scriptures are very explicit when it comes to our enemy the devil, and him afflicting us physically. In the book of Job, it tells us that it was the devil who attacked Job with boils, killed his children, and stole his property.

Job 2:7 So went Satan forth from the presence of the Lord, and smote Job with sore boils from the sole of his foot unto his crown.

Jesus came to destroy the works of the devil according to 1John 3:8, and Acts 10:38.

1 John 3:8 He that committeth sin is of the devil; for the devil sinneth from the beginning. For this purpose the Son of God was manifested, that he might destroy the works of the devil.

Acts 10:38 How God anointed Jesus of Nazareth with the Holy Ghost and with power: who went about doing good, and healing all that were oppressed of the devil; for God was with him.

I'm telling you right now that it is the thief (the devil) who comes to destroy us with sickness, diseases, and afflictions, and as long as we are in this world we are going to be having to battle the enemy. So the **fourth** step you must take is to always, and foremost exalt Christ above all else. Meditating upon the realities of Matthew, Mark, Luke, and John, is the best way to begin to exalt Christ in your heart and mind. You must begin to devour Matthew, Mark, Luke, and John, and as you read the four Gospels, and make sure you use a yellow highlighter in order to highlight every time you see that Jesus healed someone.

CHAPTER FIVE

#5 Jesus Paid the Ultimate Price!

Jesus paid the ultimate price for our healing, yours, and mine. There are so many Scriptures that we could look at pertaining to this wonderful truth, that by his stripes you were healed. Yes, there has been times when the manifestation of my healing seemed like it would never come, there has been many times when it looked like I was going to die, but I knew, that I knew, that I knew by the stripes of Jesus I was healed.

Isaiah 53:4-5 Surely he hath borne our griefs, and carried our sorrows: yet we did esteem him stricken, smitten of God, and afflicted. But he was wounded for our transgressions, he was bruised for our iniquities: the chastisement of our peace was upon him; and with his stripes we are healed.

1 Peter 2:24 Who his own self bare our sins in his own body on the tree, that we, being dead to sins, should live unto righteousness: by whose stripes ye were healed.

As I read and meditated upon these Scriptures, something wonderful happened within my heart, and mind. I experienced a great and overwhelming sorrow in my heart, and in my soul, and at that very moment I saw the terrible pain, the agony that Jesus Christ, the son of the living God, went through for my personal healing. In my heart, and in my soul I saw that Jesus had taken my sicknesses, and my diseases. It is my heart's desire that as you read this chapter you to might also experience this revelation of the sufferings of Christ, for your healing, and your deliverance. That you would no longer allow the devil to rob you from that which has already been purchased for you by the stripes, and the sufferings of Jesus Christ.

When God gave me this revelation, revealed to me by the Scriptures, I experienced a great an overwhelming love for the son of God, recognizing the price he had paid for my healing. It was like an open vision in which I saw my precious **Lord and Savior** tied to the whipping post. I saw the Roman soldiers striking, beating, and whipping the back of Jesus with the cat of nine tails. This was a Roman whip which had nine long strands, coated with oil, and covered with glass, metal shards, and sharp objects. In this vision I saw the flesh and the blood of my precious Savior splashing everything within a 10-foot radius, with each terrible stroke of the Romans soldier's whip hitting his body.

As I saw this open vision, (as I was on my knees in prayer) I wept because I knew that this horrendous beating he was enduring was for my healing, and my deliverance. To this day, even after 40 years, whenever I retell this story, great love, and sorrow still fills my heart for what Christ had to endure for me. This is the reason why I am so aggressive in my fight to receive healing. Still I have great joy, wonderful peace, and enthusiasm in this battle, because I know that by the **stripes of Jesus Christ I am healed**. This amazing price that he paid (God in the flesh)was not only for me, but for every believer who has received Christ as their Lord and Savior.

1 Timothy 3:16 And without controversy great is the mystery of godliness: God was manifest in the flesh, justified in the Spirit, seen of angels, preached unto the Gentiles, believed on in the world, received up into glory.

I am sad to say though that many within the body of Christ have not had this revelation of divine healing provided to them by the sufferings of Jesus, and still to this day are being continually afflicted by sickness, and diseases, which are caused by the devil.

*WHY PEOPLE ARE SICK (Smith Wigglesworth)

Where people are in sickness you find most times that they are in darkness about biblical, and scriptural truth. They usually know three scriptures though. They know about Paul's thorn in the flesh, and that Paul told Timothy to take a little wine for his stomach's sake, and that Paul left someone sick somewhere; they forget his name, and don't remember the name of the place, and don't know where the chapter is. Most people think they have a thorn in the flesh. The chief thing in dealing with a person who is sick is to locate their exact position. As you are ministering under the Spirit's power the Lord will let you see just that which will be more helpful and most faith-inspiring to them.

Once God imparts to you the revelation of the price that Christ paid for your healing and deliverance, your days of confusion are over with. Christ said: you will know the truth, and the truth will make you free.

My Burned Out Vocal Cords Healed (1979)

My wife and I were attending Rhema Bible Training Center. We had arrived in Oklahoma with a Ford F250 four-wheel drive but now that school was about finished, we had to make a choice. What would be the best vehicle for us to travel in? We determined that we should sell the truck, pay the bills and buy an old work van. The van that we bought needed much work: mechanical, exterior and interior. We covered the inside of the van with carpet, building a bed all the way in the back so that when we were traveling, we would not need to get a hotel. The day after graduation we had the van loaded and were headed back to Pennsylvania. There was only one major problem. The engine compartment was part way on the inside of the van and the valve covers were allowing oil to leak on top of the engine. This caused burning smoke to come inside the cabin. I determined that I could wait till I arrived in Pennsylvania to repair this problem.

The smoke was filling the cabin to the point where I had to roll down the driver and passenger windows part way in order to breathe. My wife was all right because she stayed in the back of the van lying on the bed. There was just no way that I could avoid the fumes. I breathed them in all the way from Broken Arrow, Oklahoma to Mukwonago Wisconsin to visit relatives. Then we traveled from Wisconsin to Mount Union, Pennsylvania. Over 1400 miles I drove that old van breathing in those fumes. Close to 20 hours altogether.

You can imagine what kind of condition I was in by the time we arrived at our final destination. My lungs and my throat were burnt raw. I was having a hard time breathing and I could not speak. I naturally assumed that this would remedy itself within a few days but I could not have been more wrong. Being a preacher of the gospel, one of the most important tools at my disposal is my voice.

Ever since the Lord had healed me of my speech impediment (I had been born tongue-tied), it was seldom that I was ever quiet. I was always sharing Christ, preaching and sharing what Jesus had done for me. But now, I could only speak or preach for probably less than 10 minutes before my voice was gone. During this time, I would cry out to God in a whisper asking him to help me and to restore my voice. This went on for what seemed to be months with very little results. You see, I was making the same mistake that many people are making today. I did not need to ask God to heal me because of the fact that He had already done it 2000 years ago. What I needed to do was to take authority over this physical affliction, command it to go and for my voice to be healed. I needed to command my vocal cords to be strong and healthy.

Beloved saints, we need to believe God to become impervious to destruction and damage. Impervious to destruction? What do I mean by that statement? Did not Jesus declare that He gave us power over the enemy and that nothing shall by any means come to harm us? I am not suggesting that we tempt the Lord by doing foolish things but when we get into situations like this, we need to take the authority that we have in Jesus' name and take what belongs to us because of what Christ accomplished for us.

After a while I finally got fed up, disgusted and angry with this throat and voice condition. I did not get angry with God but with the devil, and with myself for putting up with it. You need to know who your enemy really is. Even if you're the one who opened the door for the enemy, you can repent of your stupidity and ask God to forgive you and thereby receive forgiveness by faith. After you do this, it's time to go to war in order to take what is rightfully yours. Maybe some would be curious why I did not run to the medical world? The truth of the matter is that I see sickness, disease and infirmity as a spiritual condition. If I deal with it in the spiritual, then it will be dealt with in the natural.

After one particular Sunday service when I had once again lost my voice, I finally put my foot down. I first went to the Father in prayer in the name of Jesus. I spoke to the Father about all of the promises of healing, that I was a child of God and that healing was a part of the covenant He had made with me. I knew that even in the old covenant, healing was available for God's people. I was not doing this because I thought that the Lord needed to be reminded. I was doing it to build up my own faith in light of the reality of my rights as a child of God. After a while, I perceived in my heart that it was time to address the enemy about my throat and my vocal cords. I took the name of Jesus, speaking His Name in a whisper, and commanded my body to be healed and the works of the enemy to cease. Once I had finished along this line, from that moment forward with a whisper I began to praise God and worship His Name, thanking Him that I was healed. No ifs, an or buts, I was healed. From that moment forward, no matter how I felt, I kept thanking God that I was healed.

This was not something that I went about broadcasting to anybody else. As far as I was concerned, from that moment forward I was healed! For the next couple days, I just kept thanking the Lord over and over even though I could barely speak with a whisper. I was not trying to convince God or myself of this reality. I just knew, that I knew, that I knew that I was healed. A number of days went by when I woke up one morning with all of the symptoms gone. For the last 37 years I have been able to preach like a house on fire and very seldom ever lose my voice. It is the reality that "by His stripes we were healed" that gives us the victory!

Galatians 3:13 Christ hath redeemed us from the curse of the law, being made a curse for us: for it is written, Cursed is every one that hangeth on a tree:

Christ's was made a curse for us that we might be made free from the curse of the law. Jesus took our pains, and bore our sicknesses. He was wounded for our transgressions, and by his stripes we are healed. **Right Now** we are healed by the stripes of Jesus. God is not a man that he should lie, nor the son of man that he should repent. To a person who doesn't understand how faith in Christ works this will be confusing. To a person with who has not had a revelation (faith is a revelation of God's will, quickened to your heart) of the price that Jesus Christ paid for our healing, this will not make any sense. By faith you need to see that every sickness, and every disease is not from heaven, but from the devil.

Acts 10:38 How God anointed Jesus of Nazareth with the Holy Ghost and with power: who went about doing good, and healing all that were oppressed of the devil; for God was with him.

Most believers believe that when they gave their hearts to Christ that all of their sins which they had committed up to that time were instantly and completely forgiven. There forgiveness is not based on how they feel, or if anyone else agrees or disagrees with them. Of course I can go back into the sin which I have repented of, but then I will need to once again repent of it. If we take a closer look at first Peter 2:24 we will discover that sin and sickness is covered in the same Scripture.

1 Peter 2:23 Who, when he was reviled, reviled not again; when he suffered, he threatened not; but committed himself to him that judgeth righteously:24 Who his own self bare our sins in his own body on the tree, that we, being dead to sins, should live unto righteousness: by whose stripes ye were healed.

The question becomes how do we acquire, or walk in righteousness. We do it by faith in Christ Jesus by believing and trusting in his fulfilled and accomplished work. This is exactly the same way how we apprehend the divine healing that Christ has already purchased for us in his sufferings, death, and resurrection. It is all discovered in one wonderful package of salvation and redemption by the blood, the stripes, the agonies, the sufferings, the death, and the resurrection of Jesus Christ. May God give us the revelation that we are healed, and not that we are going to be healed. 99% of the time I walk out my healing before I ever see a physical manifestation of it.

How God Miraculously Healed My Broken Back

I share these stories, my personal experiences, hoping that they will give you an insight in how to receive healing, even in the most difficult situations. Now in the winter of 1977, I was working at the Belleville Feed & Grain Mill. My job was to pick up the corn, wheat, and oats from the farmers, and bring it to the mill. There it would be mixed and combined with other products for the farmers' livestock.

One cold, snowy day, the owner of the feed mill told me to deliver a load of cattle feed to an Amish farm. It was an extremely bad winter that year, with lots of snow. I was driving an International 1600 Lodestar. I backed up as far as I could to this Amish man's barn without getting stuck. The Amish never had their lanes plowed in those days, and they most likely still do not. I was approximately seventy-five feet away from his barn, which meant that I had to carry the bags at least seventy-five feet. I think there were about eighty bags of feed, with each bag weighing approximately one hundred pounds. During those years I only weighed about 130 pounds.

I would carry one bag on each of my shoulders, stumbling and pushing my way through the heavy, deep snow to get up the steep incline into the barn. Then I would stack the bags in a dry location. As usual, nobody came out to help me. Many a time when delivering things to the farms, the Amish would watch me work without lending a helping hand. About the third trip, something frightening happened to me as I was carrying two one-hundred-pound bags upon my shoulders. I felt the bones in my back snap. Something drastic just happened. I fell to the ground at that very moment almost completely crippled. I could barely move. I was filled with intense overwhelming pain.

I had been spending a lot of my time meditating in the Word of God. Every morning, I would get up about 5:00 a.m. to study. I had one of those little bread baskets with memorization scriptures in it. I believe you can still buy them to this day at a Christian bookstore. Every morning I would memorize from three to five of them. It would not take me very long, so all day long I would be meditating on these verses.

The very minute I fell down, immediately I cried out to Jesus, asking him to forgive me for my pride, and for being so stupid in carrying two hundred pounds on my little frame. After I asked Jesus to forgive me, I commanded my back to be healed in the name of Jesus Christ of Nazareth. Since I believed I was healed, I knew that I had to act now upon my faith. Please understand that I was full of tremendous pain, but I had declared that I was healed by the stripes of Jesus. The Word of God came out of my mouth as I tried to get up and then fell back down.

Even though the pain was more intense than I can express, I kept getting back up speaking the name of Jesus, then I would fall back down again. I fell down more times than I can remember. After some time I was able to take a couple steps, then I would fall again. This entire time I was saying, "In the name of Jesus, in the name of Jesus, in the name of Jesus." I finally was able to get to the truck. I said to myself if I believe I'm healed then I will unload this truck in the name of Jesus. Of course, I did not have a cell phone in order to call for help and the Amish did not own any phones on their property. Now, even if they would have had a phone, I would not have called for help. I had already called upon my help, and His name was Jesus Christ. I knew in my heart that by the stripes of Jesus I was healed. I then pulled a bag off of the back of the truck, with it falling on top of me. I would drag it a couple feet, and then fall down.

Tears were running down my face as I spoke the Word of God over and over. By the time I was done with all of the bags, the sun had already gone down. Maybe six or seven hours had gone by. I painstakingly pulled myself up into that big old 1600 Lodestar. It took everything within me to shift gears, pushing in the clutch, and driving it. I had to sit straight like a board all the way.

I finally got back to the feed mill late in the evening. Everybody had left for home a long time ago with the building being locked up. I struggled out of the Lodestar and stumbled and staggered over to my Ford pickup. I got into my pickup, and made it back to the converted chicken house. I went back to my cold, unheated, plywood floor room. It took everything in me to get my clothes off. It was a very rough and long night.

The next morning when I woke up, I was so stiff that I could not bend in the least. I was like a board. Of course, I was not going to miss work, because by the stripes of Jesus I was healed. In order to get out of bed, I had to literally roll off the bed, hitting the floor. Once I had hit the floor, it took everything for me to push myself back up into a sitting position. The tears were rolling down my face as I put my clothes and shoes on, which in itself was a miracle. I did get to work on time, though every step was excruciatingly painful. Remember, I was only twenty-one at the time, but I knew what faith was and what it wasn't. I knew that I was healed no matter how it looked, that by the stripes of Jesus Christ I was healed.

When I got to work I did not tell my boss that I had been seriously hurt the day before. I walked into the office trying to keep the pain off of my face. For some reason he did not ask me what time I made it back to work. I did not tell him to change the time clock for me in order to be paid for all of the hours I was out on the job. They had me checked out at the normal quitting time. (The love of money is what causes a lot of people not to get healed.) My boss gave me an order for feed that needed to be delivered to a local farmer. If you have ever been to a feed and grain mill, you know that there is a large shoot where the feed comes out. After it has been mixed, you have to take your feed bag, and hold it up until it's filled. It creates tremendous strain on your arms and your back, even if you're healthy.

As I was filling the bag, it almost felt like I was going to pass out, because I was in tremendous pain. Now, I'm simply saying, "In the name of Jesus, in the name of Jesus, in the name of Jesus" under my breath. The second bag was even more difficult than the first bag, but I kept on saying, "In the name of Jesus." I began on the third bag and as I was speaking the name of Jesus, the power of God hit my back and I was instantly and completely, totally healed from the top of my head, to the tip of my toes. I was healed as I went on my way. My place of employment never did know what had happened to me. That has been 38 years ago, and my back is still healed by the stripes of Christ to this day.

CHAPTER SIX

#6 God Wants You Healed!

This is the **sixth** element, principal, reality involved in your healing. The very **first** step was that you need to get into the realm of faith. The **second** step is that you must be desperate, determined, extremely serious when it comes to receiving your healing. The **third** reality I shared with you was that you **must never exalt**, boast or brag about the affliction that is attacking you. The Bible literally fore warns us that we will experience many trials, and afflictions, tribulations in this lifetime. We overcome every one of these by the promises that God has made available to us, by faith in Christ.

Psalm 34:19Many are the afflictions of the righteous: but the Lord delivereth him out of them all.

Psalm 34:17 The righteous cry, and the Lord heareth, and delivereth them out of all their troubles.

Psalm 34:4 I sought the Lord, and he heard me, and delivered me from all my fears.

Acts 14:22 Confirming the souls of the disciples, and exhorting them to continue in the faith, and that we must through much tribulation enter into the kingdom of God.

Hebrews 11:33 Who through faith subdued kingdoms, wrought righteousness, obtained promises, stopped the mouths of lions.

The **fourth** reality, principal, step is that you must always exalt Christ even in the mist of the trial. The **fifth** step is that you need to have a revelation of the price that Jesus Christ paid for your redemption. That Christ himself has paid the ultimate price for your healing, and therefore the devil has no right to afflict your body any longer. Remember all of these steps, principles, realities are based upon the truth of God's word, and the fact that it is impossible for God to lie. That he is the Father of lights in whom there is no variableness neither shadow of turning.

Hebrews 6:18 That by two immutable things, in which it was impossible for God to lie, we might have a strong consolation, who have fled for refuge to lay hold upon the hope set before us:

Titus 1:2 In hope of eternal life, which God, that cannot lie, promised before the world began;

Numbers 23:19 God is not a man, that he should lie; neither the son of man, that he should repent: hath he said, and shall he not do it? or hath he spoken, and shall he not make it good?

The **sixth** step that we are going to look at is **"God Wants You Healed"**. Actually God wants you to be healed way more than you want to be healed. God wants all of us to be fruitful, productive, prosperous, healthy, and overcoming in every area of our lives. How do we know this? By his word, and the price which he paid for our salvation. The fact that he is the one who created us, and at the very beginning he gave to us an amazing commission discovered in Genesis chapter 1.

Genesis 1:28 And God blessed them, and God said unto them, Be fruitful, and multiply, and replenish the earth, and subdue it: and have dominion over the fish of the sea, and over the fowl of the air, and over every living thing that moveth upon the earth.

The Scriptures declare that healing is the bread of the children of God, those who are born again, washed in the blood of Jesus Christ. Not only does God want his children to be healed, but God wants all of humanity to be healed, saved, and delivered. God would have all men to come to the knowledge of salvation, that they might be washed in his blood, born again, filled with his spirit, and walking in his divine nature.

2 Peter 3:9 The Lord is not slack concerning his promise, as some men count slackness; but is longsuffering to us-ward, not willing that any should perish, but that all should come to repentance.

Many times I have prayed for sinners, the unconverted to be healed in the name of Jesus Christ of Nazareth, and God gloriously healed them. **You might ask: why did God heal them?** Because God is a loving and caring creator. Now, if God would heal these people who have no interest in him whatsoever, will he not heal those who cry out to him day and night? The answer to this question is: **Yes, Yes, Yes!** I would like to share with you a number of experiences I have had in praying for those who did not want, or know God.

The Huntington County Fair (1980)

My vacation time was coming up as a pastor and I had two weeks in the summer time. The Spirit of God had quickened to my heart to put a tent up at the Huntington County Fair. I began to investigate where I could get a tent. I was informed that another Christian group had a campground in Roxbury, Pennsylvania, and that they would rent you a tent for a very good price. I was able to reach them and gave them the dates I wanted to rent their tent. I made arrangements to pick the rental tent up. The tent I was going to rent would seat two hundred people. Next I contacted people in Huntington to find out who the coordinator of the Huntington Fair was. When I finally got his number, I called him up. He informed me all of the spaces were filled in advance for two years ahead of time. I was not worried because it wasn't my responsibility to make it happen. If I had truly heard from God, then all I had to do was my part, God would do the rest. I did not tell this person that they had to give me a place because God told me. I simply asked him to speak to the personnel who made these decisions. When he came back, he said they had an empty space they always kept open for people who wanted to have picnics. It was right next to the Þre department's bingo stand. They said if we wanted to put up a gospel tent we could use that particular area. Praise God for His favor! God did awesome things under that tent in that week.

Unbelieving Man Healed

One day as I was preaching in the tent, a man who looked to be in his mid-thirties was hobbling by really slow on a pair of crutches. He was not even looking in the direction of our tent, but was looking straight ahead, minding his own business. As I looked at him, the Spirit of God quickened the gift of faith inside of me. When God quickens my heart in this way I do not even think what I'm about to do. I simply act upon the quickening and the witness in my heart. I found myself calling out to this particular man, speaking over the microphone system. Everybody could hear me within a hundred feet, if not further. Probably the whole Huntington Fair could hear us! (Actually the fire department was really upset with us because we were disturbing their bingo games.) I called out to this man but he ignored me. Once again I challenged him to come into the tent so God could heal him. This time he looked my way but kept hobbling along. I called out the third time, encouraging him to come and be healed of his problem.

After the third time, he finally came into the tent. When he came to the front, I asked him if he had faith to believe that God would heal him. He looked at me as if I had lost my mind. He was probably thinking, *You're the one who called me up here. I don't even know what this is about. Everybody was staring at me, so I had to come!* He did not respond to my question. I told him that I was going to pray for him now and God would heal him! I asked him again if he believed this. Once again he did not respond. Then I laid my hands on him and commanded his leg to be healed In the name of Jesus Christ of Nazareth.

After I was done praying, I told him to put down his crutches and start walking without them. He stood there staring at me. Everybody else was also staring at me. This was okay because the gift of faith was at work in my heart. I reached forward and took away his crutches. I threw them on the ground and spun him around. When I'm in this realm I'm not thinking, I'm simply acting. Then I pushed him, and he stumbled forward and began to walk toward the back of the tent. He was picking his legs high up in the air, high stepping it. When he got to the edge of the tent he spun back toward me. Tears were streaming from his eyes and down his cheeks. He came back toward me walking perfectly normal with no limp whatsoever!

I gave him the microphone, and asked him to tell us what did God do for him. He kept saying, "You don't understand" over and over. Once again, I encouraged him to tell us his story. I had him face the people in that tent and those outside of the tent who had been watching. He told us that last winter he had been walking on a very icy sidewalk and he lost his footing. Slipping and sliding, he fell forward onto the concrete and ice. He fell down so hard on his kneecap that he had done something terrible to it. He could not move his knee whatsoever, and it was extremely painful. He went to the doctor's office and they x-rayed it. The x-rays revealed that his kneecap had literally been shattered and destroyed. In just two more days he was scheduled to have a major operation to replace his kneecap.

I encouraged him to go back to his doctor and get it x-rayed again, and to come back and tells us the doctors report. Sure enough, a couple days later he came back to the tent giving a wonderful testimony. He had gone to his doctor. He said when he walked into the doctor's office they could tell that his knee was normal. The doctor asked him what had happened. He told them about the encounter he had with Jesus at our tent meeting. They x-rayed his kneecap and discovered he had a brand-new kneecap!

God Heals a Mafia Man's Eyes! (2013)

I have a house where I take in and keep single men. Some of these men come from real rough backgrounds. I had one such gentleman that I was renting to who was quite large and intimidating. I would try to share Christ with him whenever the opportunity arrived, but he was so liberal in his thinking that it did not seem to be having any impact upon him. Everything I believe that is wrong, he proclaimed was right. And everything that I believe is right, he would argue against.

He informed me that in his past he had worked for the Mafia, and at one time he was what they called a THUMPER! I asked him what he meant by a thump-er? He said that he had never physically murdered anyone, but that they would send him to rough up people, you know thump them! I have no doubt at all that what he told me was true.

One day as I was at the house where I keep these men, I saw him standing in the main front room. He seemed quite upset and distressed. I asked him what was wrong. He informed me that he had just come from the doctors because he had been having terrible problems with his eyes. After the Doctor had conducted all of the test they came back with a very disturbing report. They informed him that he had an eye disease (long medical term) that was going to cause him to go blind.

At that moment the spirit of God rose up with in me as he told me this, and I proclaimed boldly that in the name of Jesus Christ he was not going to go blind. I told him: **close your eyes**! He said what? I said: **close your eyes**! He shut his eyes, and I took my two thumbs and laid them forcefully over his two eyelids. I declared: in the **name of Jesus Christ** you lying spirit of infirmity, come out of these eyes right now! **Be healed in Jesus name**! I then removed my thumbs from his eyelids, he looked at me with questioning eyes. I said to him: it's done! He said what? I said it is done. You are healed in the name of Jesus. He said: really? I said: yes Christ has made you whole. It seemed for a minute that tears formed in his eyes as I turned around and walked away.

Approximately a week later he showed up at a thrift store that we manage and operate. He walked into the store asking for Pastor Mike. They informed him that I was not there at the time. Tears were rolling down his face, and they asked him what they could do for him. He told them with great joy and excitement that he had gone back to the doctors, and that his eyes were completely healed. He started hugging the people that where they're running the store. This large ex-Mafia thumper gave his heart to Jesus Christ that day, and became a part of the church I pastor.

Deaf man's ear healed! (2014)

As I was saying I rent rooms to single men at a boarding house. A brand-new tenant moved in to one of the rooms. Because it was the Fourth of July I could not get together with him until the next day. He texted me that night with a request, informing me that he had to get free from a demonic ENTITY! He asked if I could possibly help him with this situation. As far as I know he did not know that I was a minister. I asked him if he had taken the name of Jesus Christ to this ENTITY (not really knowing whether he believed in Christ)? He responded by texting that in no way would he ever use that name, because he was too afraid to.

The next morning at approximately 9 o'clock I arrived at the house to meet him, and his name was Todd. He was a man about my age and my height, who turned out to be a construction worker who builds houses. I asked him to tell me his story, that is about this entity. He informed me that his grandmother was involved in some kind of Satanic activity, and at the age of nine these demonic powers began to oppress him, literally physically shoving him many times into the walls. As a young man he eventually became an alcoholic because he was using the alcohol to try to suppress these attacks, and the fear that came upon him. Actually the opposite of what he wanted happened, and instead of getting better he just got worse, and eventually ending up in trouble.

He was now approximately 58 years old, and it had been going on for almost 50 years. He had tried to get relief but nothing seemed to help. As he began to get older he tried to get rid of the fear that would come upon him by drinking heavily. This of course made things much worse. He said that just two years ago he had ended up drunk while he was driving his motorcycle. This resulted in him having a terrible and life-threatening accident. In this motorcycle accident his head injury was so bad that it had left him completely blind in his left eye, and deaf in his left ear.

The medical world informed him there was no help for his eye or his ear because of his head injury that he experienced in a motorcycle accident. In his left eye there was no pupil, and nothing to be seen but white. He also informed me that for the last two years his left ear had absolutely no discernible sound but a constant irritating hissing.

I shared my testimony with Todd about how God had delivered me, save my soul, and completely healed my body. I gave him my book "Living in the Realm of the Miraculous", encouraging him to read it, to build up his faith. I asked him if he had ever given his heart to Jesus Christ. He responded that he had never done such a thing, or ever been invited to do this. I then informed him that I would like to pray over him, and ask God to give him a miracle. He agreed to allow me to pray for him.

I laid my left hand over his blind eye, and my right hand over his deaf ear. I spoke the name of Jesus Christ, and commanded the blind spirit, and deaf spirit to come out right now by the authority of Christ. Then I spoke a creative miracle to his blind eye and to his death ear, commanding them to be restored in the name of Jesus Christ of Nazareth. I did not speak, or pray very loud in the name of Jesus, but I simply spoke with authority, and with the compassion of Christ for this man.

When I removed my hands from his head, he looked like he was in complete shock. He informed me that the moment I spoke in the name of Jesus that there was a loud popping sound in his left ear. He exclaimed with excitement that this was the first time he had heard any other type of noise other than the hissing sound that he had heard for the last two years. I told him to examine his hearing a little more, and then he told me with complete shock that all of the existing hissing sound was completely gone.

I had him cover his good ear with his left hand. Then I bent down to his ear, and whispered the name of Jesus approximately four times. He did not know exactly what I was saying, but would say Yesis, repeatedly. Then I began to say other things in his ear, which caused him to begin to literally cry and shake. He could not believe it, but God had opened up his ear, and repairable his damaged left deaf ear.

I shared the gospel with him in a much deeper way now that I had is complete and total undivided attention. When I was done speaking the reality of Christ to him I asked him if he would like to give his heart to Jesus Christ? He told me that he was ready to not only accept Christ, but to surrender his life to him. He was shaking under the power of God as I lead him into a prayer of salvation.

He informed me that he would begin to attend our church services, and kept thank me, and hugged me twice. I informed him that it was Jesus Christ who had healed him, and made him whole, and that I was nobody special. I left him standing in his room shaking and crying saying: thank you Jesus, thank you God.

You might ask why God doesn't just instantly heal every one like these sinners that I prayed for? Before the end of this book I hope to answer that question, and other questions you might have. One thing you must realize is that as a born again believer, according to God's perspective, you **already are healed**! Yes, you understood me correctly, **you are healed**. It is a done deal because when Jesus went to the whipping post, the cross of Calvary, and breathed his last breath, and said it is finished, it was done! Our redemption is a completed work that we by faith must receive, accept, confess, and act upon accordingly. This is the realm of faith that we must learn to walk in , live in, move in, breathe in, and speak in. This walk does not just come automatically any more than it does for a newborn child who has to learn how to do all that a developed and mature full grown man does.

Another aspect of God wanting us healed is revealed in the fact that our bodies are now the temples, the tabernacles, the house, the dwelling place of the Holy Ghost. This body we live in, and move in, has been created by God, purchased, redeemed, and ransomed by Jesus Christ. Once you begin to understand that you belong to God, and that you are the caretaker of the body which is God's property, your whole perspective on life will change. I fight the fight of faith when it comes to my physical, mental, and emotional well-being based upon the fact that I will give an account to God for this life, this body God has given to me, and that I am to be a caretaker of it.

1 Corinthians 3:16 Know ye not that ye are the temple of God, and that the Spirit of God dwelleth in you?

1 Corinthians 6:19 Do you not know that your bodies are temples of the Holy Spirit, who is in you, whom you have received from God? You are not your own;

1 Corinthians 6:15 Do you not know that your bodies are members of Christ himself? Shall I then take the members of Christ and unite them with a prostitute? Never!

2 Corinthians 5:15 And that he died for all, that they which live should not henceforth live unto themselves, but unto him which died for them, and rose again.

If you study the Scriptures, you will discover that God healed everyone that Jesus Christ prayed for. Not only did God heal everybody that Jesus prayed for, but also the disciples, including Peter. Actually Peter went so deep into the spirit that everyone that laid a sick person down in his path, where his shadow touched them, they were all instantly healed. It is God's will to heal everyone, just like it is his will that everybody comes to repentance, is born again, saved, and makes it to heaven.

I don't care what a preacher has told you, or what book you have read, or what experiences people have had, I want you to know based upon the word of God, it is God's will to heal you every single time. You might say: but I know many Christians who have not been healed. I am sorry to say that many believers have used this theology many times to rob themselves of divine healing. I know people that from all indications went to hell, but that does not mean that it was God's will for them to go to hell. Now, if a person, a believer that gets sick, dies from that sickness, or disease, it does not rob them from the blessed hope of eternal lifey with Jesus Christ.

My Sister could have Lived (2006)

I wish I could say that all of my stories end with victory, but that's not the case. God has given to all men the power of choice in order that they can choose to trust him, or not. In 1975 I introduced my sister Debbie, who was my older sister by two years, to the Lord. I also had the blessed opportunity to lead her into the baptism of the Holy Spirit. In 1983 I started Jesus Is Lord Ministries International, in the Gettysburg Pennsylvania area. My sister who was a wonderful typist and secretary came to work for me. She moved from Waukesha, Wisconsin, in order to do this. She was my secretary from 1984 to about 1994.

She had one major habit that she did not seem to want to get free from. She loved to smoke. This was a family curse that was upon my dad, mother, two brothers, my sister, and myself. I remember as we all sat around the table smoking our cigarettes, and drinking our coffee, with a large cloud of smoke hanging over us. When I gave my heart to Jesus, Christ instantly set me free from 3 1/2 packs of cigarettes a day, cigars, and chewing tobacco, in which I have been gloriously free from since 1975. The rest of my family just seemed to not be able to get free, or wanted to be free. Because my sister was my secretary, and she still had the habit of smoking, a religious spirit rose up within the congregation I was pastor of. They brought tremendous persecution because of Debbie's habit, and this is one of the major reasons why she eventually left my employment, and move back to Wisconsin.

One day she came to me with tremendous fear that she would die from cancer. She wanted me to pray that she would never get cancer, but I told her that I would love to pray for her, but she was opening the door for cancer because of her bondage to cigarettes. I told her I would love to pray for her to not only to be protected from cancer, but also to be delivered from cigarettes. She informed me that she did not want to be free from cigarettes. I knew at that moment in my heart that no good would come from this.

Debbie moved back to Wisconsin next to my brothers, and their families. Now, Debbie really loved children, but she was never able to have them because while she was in the Air Force, the medical professionals had physically damaged her by a wrong prognosis, and an operation based upon this prognosis. Whenever my family and I visited in Wisconsin, we would go to see her. In about 2004 it began to become obvious that there was something wrong with her physically. She had always been slender, but she began to lose a lot of weight. In the winter of 2006 we were contacted by one of my brothers informing us that Debbie was in a Catholic hospital. She was close to the edge of death because she was diagnosed in the last stages of cancer.

When my wife and I arrived with our four children at the hospital, one of my younger brothers was there with his wife and children. They were very close to Debbie, and were extremely upset. We went into the hospital room, and there Debbie laid in what seemed to be a coma. I wanted to lay hands on her right away to take authority over this spirit of death and cancer, but I knew in my heart with my brother and his family being so distressed, that I would have to wait. There was a spirit of extreme sorrow and sadness upon everybody who came to see Debbie, but not on my family. My wife and children have seen through the years God do the impossible, and raising people from the bed of death who were filled with cancer. We were not going to allow a spirit of fear to overwhelm us.

Through that whole day we just simply stood quietly in the hospital room, waiting room, and hallway waiting for an opportunity to pray for Debbie. We had to wait until everybody was gone. Eventually much later in the day, my local family members left to go eat, and take care of other responsibilities. The minute everybody was gone, I called my wife, three sons and daughters to the side of my sisters bed. We all knew what needed to be done. Every one of us gathered around her bed as she laid there seeming to be in a coma, laying hands upon her. As I prayed in the name of Jesus, taking authority over this spirit of cancer and death, all of my family members were in total faith. When I finished praying, there seem to be a wonderful presence of God and his peace flooding and enveloping the room. We stood around quietly around her bed talking about how wonderful Christ is, and his amazing mercy and love. As we were speaking, my precious sister Debbie opened up her eyes. Immediately it was like somebody had turned on the switch, and she smiled at us. She began to speak to us as if there hadn't been nothing wrong with her. Christ had answered our prayers, and brought her out of her coma.

She actually sat up in bed, as we propped pillows up behind her back. My family and I were filled with great joy as we saw the color of her skin change from a deathly, chalky white, to a vibrant slight pink. We all sat there laughing and talking with my sister as she communicated with us in complete awareness. Later that evening my next to youngest brother came back with his wife. He walked into the room, and saw my sister communicating and laughing with us. Now you would think that this would have caused great joy in his heart. I'm sorry to say that this was not the case. Actually he became extremely upset at us because we were laughing and talking like everything was okay. A spirit of fear had completely captured his mind, and all of the rest of my family, (outside of my wife and children). He actually took me aside, and gave me a very strong verbal rebuke for us smiling and laughing with my sister. I did not defend myself because I knew that it would be a waste of time. I also knew in my heart that if my sister did not come back to Pennsylvania with us, she would die.

When my wife and children were alone with me, I shared with them what the Lord had spoken to my heart. They were all in complete agreement with me. When we finally were able to speak to Debbie alone, I encouraged her to come home with us. We told her that we would take care of her twenty-four, seven. At that time we were living in a very nice house, with an extra bedroom, and there would be no problem with her being with us. I am sorry to say that she did not agree to come home with us because she did not want to leave my brothers children. My one brother had four children, and the other had two children, she loved very much.

The hospital had previously informed us that if she wanted to go home, she could because there was nothing more they could do for her. After we had prayed, and she had come out of this coma, the hospital had not examined her because according to their prognosis she was full of cancer, and there was no hope. We spent approximately three days with her, knowing that this would be the last time we would see her on this side of heaven. We knew that to live she would have to be wrapped in an atmosphere of faith, which she was not going to be able to get with my brothers and their families. As we were getting ready to leave, they were packing her up to go to one of my younger brothers home. My wife and I and our children hugged her, and spoke softly to her as we left. The last time that I saw Debbie she was lying there with a smile on her face. I think it was only a week later that she passed on to be with the Lord. It is so important that we surround ourselves with people of like precious faith.

CHAPTER SEVEN

#7 Examine Your Heart

The **seventh step, reality, truth** that you need to embrace to be healed is to examine your own heart. We need to make sure that we are not involved in known sin, rebellion, disobedience to God. We also need to make sure that there is not any bitterness, resentment, on forgiveness, hatred in our hearts. I am not speaking about being sinless, or even confessing that your sinless. The only sinless man that has ever walked this earth was Jesus Christ. In first John it says:

1 John 1:7 But if we walk in the light, as he is in the light, we have fellowship one with another, and the blood of Jesus Christ his Son cleanseth us from all sin.8 If we say that we have no sin, we deceive ourselves, and the truth is not in us.9 If we confess our sins, he is faithful and just to forgive us our sins, and to cleanse us from all unrighteousness.

I am speaking about open rebellion to God. I'm saying if you're going to have full confidence in your prayers being answered, receiving your Healing, you must make sure that your heart is right with God. If you discover that there are things in your life that is contrary to God's will when it comes to your own personal decisions, then you simply need to repent, confess your sins to Christ, and turn away from your wicked deeds. God will be faithful, and just to forgive you of all of your unrighteousness.

Once you confess and repent of your sins do not think for a moment that automatically the enemy will leave you alone. The demonic world is similar to that of nasty little gnats swarming around your head constantly aggravating, and attacking you. It is like when you or I are walking through a woods, a forest in the summertime. Before you know what is happening these pesky, nasty little gnats, horse flies begin to show up buzzing around your head. These nasty little insects just will not leave you alone, especially when you're sweating, or you're out there splitting wood. You cannot go by how you feel when you are standing on God's word for your Forgiveness, and your Healing.

The enemy will tell you that God has not forgiven you even though you have repented, confessed, and turned away from the sins in the sincerity of your heart. I tell people it is like a skunk that has been killed. The skunk is dead, but the stink will still hang around for a while. After you have examined your heart, and confessed your sins, then you can come **boldly** before the throne of grace in your time of need to obtain mercy, and find grace to help in overcoming these sins.

Hebrews 4:15 For we have not an high priest which cannot be touched with the feeling of our infirmities; but was in all points tempted like as we are, yet without sin.16 Let us therefore come boldly unto the throne of grace, that we may obtain mercy, and find grace to help in time of need.

One of the greatest attributes about God is that he is merciful, and his mercy is new every morning. The **seventh step, reality, truth** is that you must examine your heart making sure there is no sin in your heart, no bitterness, no resentment, no hate towards anyone that might have hurt you in any way, or your loved ones. This is a very serious area that must be dealt with in our lives. You see God boldly declares that if you will not forgive others, then God will not forgive you.

Matthew 6:15 But if ye forgive not men their trespasses, neither will your Father forgive your trespasses.

The Scriptures dealing with the subject of forgiveness, and forgiving others must be taken very seriously.

God means what he says, and says what he means!

Never think for a moment that because God is love, and is full of compassion, and mercy that it overrides what he has proclaimed, declared as truth. Based upon the reality of the Scriptures we can see immediately that the doctrine of Calvinism, OSAS, (Once Saved Always Saved) Is a deception propagated by the devil. Un-forgiveness in our hearts is a decision that we make. We knowingly, and purposely choose not to forgive someone who has done us wrong, or we believe they have committed a wrong. God boldly declares that he is the only one that has the right to not forgive.

Luke 6:37 Judge not, and ye shall not be judged: condemn not, and ye shall not be condemned: forgive, and ye shall be forgiven:

You might say that unforgiveness is the unpardonable sin, that is until you forgive from the heart. Now, this is very serious because God says **if you do not forgive** from your heart, then all of **your sins are placed back onto you**. Basically if you do not forgive from your heart than what Christ did on the cross for you, absolutely will not help you in any regards. This truth will set you free from the deception of Calvinism. A person who's sins are not forgiven cannot, and will not go to heaven!

Matthew 18:34 And his lord was wroth, and delivered him to the tormentors, till he should pay all that was due unto him.35 So likewise shall my heavenly Father do also unto you, if ye from your hearts forgive not everyone his brother their trespasses.

SMITHS WIGGLESWORTH RESPONSE TO CALVINISM

God says to us, "In patience possess thy soul." How beautiful! There have been in England great churches which believed once saved always saved. I thank God that they are all disappearing. You will find if you go to England those hardheaded people that used to hold on to these things are almost gone. Why? Because they went on to say whatever you did, if you were elect, you were right. That is so wrong. The elect of God are those that keep pressing forward. The elect of God cannot hold still. They are always on the move. Every person that has a knowledge of the elect of God realizes it is important that he continues to press forward. He cannot endure sin nor darkness's nor things done in the shadows. The elect is so in earnest to be right for God that he burns every bridge behind him.

"Knowing this, that first there shall be a falling away"

Knowing this, that first God shall bring into His treasury the realities of the truth and put them side by side — the false, and the true, those that can be shaken in mind, and those that cannot be shaken in mind. God requires us to be so built upon the foundation of truth that we cannot be shaken in our mind, it doesn't matter what comes.

THE 10 COMMANDMENTS ARE DONE AWAY WITH!

"Done away! Done away!" Henceforth there is a new cry in our hearts, "I delight to do Thy will, O God." He taketh away the first, the ministration of death, written and engrave in stones, that He might establish the second, this ministration of righteousness, this life in the Spirit. You ask, "Does a man who is filled with the Spirit cease to keep the commandments?" I simply repeat what the Spirit of God has told us here, that this ministration of death, written and engrave in stones (and you know that the ten commandments were written on stones) is "DONE AWAY."

The man who becomes a living epistle of Christ, written with the Spirit of the living God, has ceased to be an adulterer, or a murderer or a covetous man; the will of God is his delight. I love to do the will of God; there is no irksomeness to it; it is no trial to pray; no trouble to read the Word of God; it is not a hard thing to go to the place of worship. With the psalmist you say, "I was glad when they said unto me, Let us go into the house of the Lord."

How does this new life work out? The thing works out because: *God works in you to will and to do of His own good pleasure (Phil. 2:13)*. There is a great difference between a pump and a spring. The law is a pump, the Baptism is a spring. The old pump gets out of order, the parts perish, and the well runs dry. The letter killeth. But the spring is ever bubbling up and there is a ceaseless flow direct from the throne of God. There is life.

It is written of Christ, *"Thou lovest righteousness, and hatest wickedness."* And in this new life in the Spirit, in this new covenant life, you love the things that are right and pure and holy, and shudder at all things that are wrong. Jesus was able to say, "The prince of this world cometh, and bath nothing in Me," and the moment we are filled with the Spirit of God we are brought into like wonderful condition, and, as we continue to be filled with the Spirit, the enemy cannot have an inch of territory in us.

Scriptures also imply that in order for us to be delivered from evil, we must forgive others their trespasses. At the same time realize that when you forgive someone of something evil they have committed, it does not automatically mean that you ignore the potential of them committing the same evil act again. An example of this would be a person who has been a pedophile. If a particular person has sexually molested a child, yes you must forgive them from your heart, but you do not allow your child, children to be put into a possible reoccurring scenario with this person. Yes, from your heart you have forgiven the person, and yet you still protect your loved ones.

To Forgive does not Always mean to forget!

You do remember the transaction that transpired, but you harbor no resentment or hatred in your heart towards that person. I have had to forgive myself many times when I have transgressed against God, after asking God for his forgiveness, and to cleanse me from all unrighteousness. Still even though I know I'm forgiven, I still remember the things that I had done wrong. I use these experiences to safeguard me from committing the same stupid decisions that I had previously made.

Luke 11:4 And forgive us our sins; for we also forgive every one that is indebted to us. And lead us not into temptation; but deliver us from evil.

You must also realize that it is not your job to examine anyone else's heart, but to know them by their fruit. It is imperative that you are not trying to change anyone, or make anyone do the will of God. I am not speaking about the fact of disciplining your children, or bringing correction, and direction, in meekness if you are in a position of authority. The enemy of our soul loves it when he gets us into a position of examining and taking the position of a judge when it comes to other people's lives. If you are being judgmental, faultfinding, critical, attacking, or speaking evil of others behind their backs, or even to their faces, it will be very difficult for you to get healed.

James 4: Speak not evil one of another, brethren. He that speaketh evil of his brother, and judgeth his brother, speaketh evil of the law, and judgeth the law: but if thou judge the law, thou art not a doer of the law, but a judge.12 There is one lawgiver, who is able to save and to destroy: who art thou that judgest another?

It is so easy to be deceived into thinking that there is nothing wrong in your life, your attitude, and your responses to circumstances, and people when in all reality you are way out in left field. As the old saying goes: **you're so deep into the woods that you can't see the forest.** There have been times when my wife, or my children kept telling me that I had issues. The pride in my heart would not let me acknowledge, or even see what they were saying was true. One day I'm in my office, and I'm just sitting there quietly speaking to the Lord.

It came to my mind to asked the Lord if I had any issues in my life, as my wife and children were implying that I was not right in certain areas? I had a clipboard sitting in front of me with writing paper on it. The minute I asked the Lord if there was anything in my life that was not right. immediately HE began to speak to my heart. He began to show me things that I thought, I said, and I was doing that was not pleasing to him. I began to write down what was coming to my heart. To my utter shock and amazement before I knew what was happening that whole piece of paper was filled from top to bottom. I sat there in complete shock realizing that the enemy had deceived me into thinking everything was okay in my life.

Now, the only way to overcome these issues that the Lord revealed to me was by the word of God. I began to find Scriptures for each of these areas, writing down their locations. Of course I had to go back to my family, repent before them, and acknowledge that they were right. As I began to apply the Scriptures in these areas of my life, God gave me victory. God wants to heal, and deliver us from every evil affliction, sickness, and disease, but we must take the necessary steps revealed to us in the word of God in order to be healed, and made whole. Now, you might ask why did not God tell you before this particular event what was wrong in your life? This simple answer is that I had not asked him to show me what was wrong with me. If you do not ask God what he thinks, his opinion, his perspective in most cases he will let you be ignorant even to your own detriment.

A Sad but True Story! (1999)

I had a former pastor one time that lead a rebellion against me in our Christian school and our church. This gentleman had been one of the teachers in our school for a number of years (he had also been a pastor of a local church) and because of a decision I had made he had become extremely angry and upset at me. He was so upset at me that he spoke to all of our school teachers, and our personnel against me.

This bitterness in his heart spread like a house on fire throughout the whole ministry. Strife, gossip, and rumors about me began to spread like an incurable disease. It became so bad that after the school year, I simply had to shut the school down. I mean it was so vicious that it was impossible to keep going with our school.

James 3:16 For where envying and strife is, there is confusion and every evil work.

During this whole conflict not one time did I ever get angry, bitter or upset with him knowing that I could not afford to be bitter. The next thing that I heard was that this dear brother had been hit with a deadly and incurable disease. I began earnestly praying for him, he had been a good pastor and teacher at one time, but had allowed the seed of bitterness to spring up in him, contaminating many others with him. One day out of the blue I received a phone call from this man's wife. She said her husband would like to speak to me. I had to press the phone tightly against my ear because he was speaking to me with barely a whisper. He asked me to please forgive him for what he had done. He said he knew he was wrong for causing all of the strife which he had caused. With tears rolling down my face I told him that he was forgiven. We spoke for a little bit longer before we both hung up. Late that same evening he passed on to be with the Lord. Praise

God for his mercy and his goodness that even when we disobey him, there is still **mercy** and forgiveness available.

Hebrews 12:15 Looking diligently lest any man fail of the grace of God; lest any root of bitterness springing up trouble you, and thereby many be defiled;

We have to be careful that a root of bitterness is not allowed in any of us. It is literally a demonic seed of unbelief which rises up against the mercy of God that we must operate in for other people, whether they are right or wrong.

WHY MANY BELIEVERS ARE NOT HEALED!
(Smith Wigglesworth)

I realize that God can never bless us on the lines of being hardhearted, critical or unforgiving. This will hinder faith quicker than anything. I remember being at a meeting where there were some people tarrying for the Baptism-seeking for cleansing, for the moment a person is cleansed the Spirit will fall. There was one man with eyes red from weeping bitterly. He said to me, "I shall have to leave. It is no good my staying without I change things. I have written a letter to my brother-in-law, and filled it with hard words, and this thing must first be straightened out." He went home and told his wife, "I'm going to write a letter to your brother and ask him to forgive me for writing to him the way I did." "You fool!" she said. "Never mind," he replied, "this is between God and me, and it has got to be cleared away." He wrote the letter and came again, and straightway God filled him with the Spirit.

I believe there are a great many people who would be healed, but they are harboring things in their hearts that are as a blight. Let these things go. Forgive, and the Lord will forgive you. There are many good people, people that mean well, but they have no power to do anything for God. There is just some little thing that came in their hearts years ago, and their faith has been paralyzed ever since. Bring everything to the light. God will sweep it all away if you will let Him. Let the precious blood of Christ cleanse from all sin. If you will but believe, God will meet you and bring into your lives the sunshine of His love.

FALSE MESSAGE OF GRACE!

Grace is one of the most misunderstood subjects of the Bible. They have confused it with the subject of God's mercy. Grace is a Greek word by which we get the word charisma. It means the **divine ability of God** at work in a believer. Paul says that by the grace of God I am what I am. He also tells us that the grace of God should not be in vain in regards to overcoming sin. Calvinism seems to have penetrated every part of the modern day church (once saved, always saved). So many are being deceived by the sloppy agape, greasy grace, I'm okay you're, okay message.

Christ did not come to leave us in our sins, defeated by the devil, and immorality. He came to give us a new nature, with victory over sin. It's amazing how many people are being deceived by this false doctrine. In the book of Revelation, JESUS never talks about grace, but he does go into great detail about works. Jesus said in the book of Revelation chapter 1 to chapter 3, I know thy works.

I think people are willingly ignorant of the importance of the works that is produced in us, because of Christ Jesus, and our faith in him, that produces obedience. no matter how many scriptures you present to some people in contexts, they will still disagree with the fact that right after chapter 2 in Ephesians were it says that we are saved by grace, it goes on to say that we are created unto **good works**. No it is not me doing the good works, but it is Christ doing them in me, and through me.

CHAPTER EIGHT

#8 Eat & Drink the Word

The Bible says in the last days that there is going to be a famine in the land. In my opinion this famine has already been manifested, and it is a famine of God's word hidden in the heart of believers. Many believers really do not understand God. They do not know how to trust God, or to look to God because there has been a lack of those in leadership who move in the realm of faith and the word. Much of the modern church leaders are successful not because of faith in **Christ, and God's word**, but simply because they are worldly wise. Using natural practical worldly wisdom to grow their local churches, and yet the Scripture declares that *man shall not live by bread alone, but by every word that proceeds out of the mouth of God.*

MOST OF THOSE WE HAVE CALLED SUCCESSFUL PASTORS ARE SIMPLY WORLDLY WISE MAN. TRUE SUCCESS IS WHEN WE SEE THE IMAGE & CHARACTER OF CHRIST BEING FORMED IN PEOPLE!

Proverbs 3:5-6 Trust in the Lord with all thine heart; and lean not unto thine own understanding. In all thy ways acknowledge him, and he shall direct thy paths.

If you read Hebrews 11 there is actually 50 events in this particular chapter. We call this chapter the faith Hall of Fame. We need to really take a good look at these men and women, and the conditions that they were experiencing. How they responded to all of these trials, tribulations and test. They overcame by faith based upon the word that God had given to them. It is a faith that works by love, and when you are walking in this realm of faith you will not worry, you will not be fearful, you will not be angry, you will not be frustrated, you will not be upset, you will not be self-centered, you will not be self-serving and self-seeking, you will not be self-pleasing! True biblical faith takes a hold of God's word, and the divine nature of **Christ,** and will not let go. When **Jesus** said that faith had made a person whole, what he was saying is: your confidence in me, in my word, and your confidence in **My Father** has made you whole. So it's your faith in **these three areas** that makes all things possible. The **eighth step, realm, reality** is that we must eat and drink the word of God. We must eat and drink the words of Christ, even as the descendants of Abraham partook of the Passover Lamb.

John 6:1 After these things Jesus went over the sea of Galilee, which is the sea of Tiberias.² And a great multitude followed him, because they saw his miracles which he did on them that were diseased.³ And Jesus went up into a mountain, and there he sat with his disciples.⁴ And the passover, a feast of the Jews, was nigh'

The **Passover** is indeed the most important festival, feast day, tradition and ceremony of the Jewish people. In order to better comprehend exactly what the **Passover** is we would have to step back into history and take a look in the book of Exodus when God had sent Moses to deliver the Israelites from the hands of Pharaoh.

God sent Moses to the Israelites in order to bring deliverance and freedom because they have been in captivity for 400 years. Of course Moses is a typology of **Jesus Christ** who came to set us free from the slavery of sin by or through the means of us having faith in **Christ, and his word.** God told Pharaoh through Moses to let his people go. We all know the story how Pharaoh refused to obey God. The Lord had Moses to bring plague after plague in order to free the people from the hands of Pharaoh. None of these plagues convinced Pharaoh to lose God's people. There was to be one last judgment, and It was the **Passover lamb.** This would be the final blow to Egypt which would release the children of God, by and through the **Passover** God would change the world. From that moment forward nothing would ever be the same. As you and

I receive revelation on the **Passover**, and what it means to us, our lives will never be the same. The **Passover** in the Bible is talked about specifically **73 times**. It talks about the **lamb** or the **Passover lamb one hundred times.** As a result of the Passover the children of Israel from that day forward (if they would believe the words of Moses) could walk in health, and receive divine healing.

Psalm 105:37 He brought them forth also with silver and gold: and there was not one feeble person among their tribes.

Exodus 15:26 And said, If thou wilt diligently hearken to the voice of the Lord thy God, and wilt do that which is right in his sight, and wilt give ear to his commandments, and keep all his statutes, I will put none of these diseases upon thee, which I have brought upon the Egyptians: for I am the Lord that healeth thee.

Did you notice that God told Moses that everyone should go and get themselves a lamb without spot or blemish? The Lord told Moses that if you obey me in the keeping of this celebration it will finally set you free from the control of the enemy! If we as believers would do likewise, with the revelation of **Christ** our **Passover lamb**, we would truly be set free. What is the **8th Way** in which we can be healed?

#8 By Eating & Drinking Jesus Christ and the word of God!

Hebrews 11:28 Through faith he kept the passover, and the sprinkling of blood, lest he that destroyed the firstborn should touch them.

Healing comes when you eat of the **Passover** by means of God's **WORD**, with a sincere heart of love and devotion. Of course the **Passover lamb** is **Jesus Christ**, the only begotten Son of God. John the Baptist had a revelation of **Jesus Christ**. When he was baptizing at the river Jordan and John saw **Jesus** walking towards him, he said: **Behold the Lamb of God Which Takes Away the Sins of the World!**

Now there were conditions that had to be met in order for the people to have a right to partake of the **Passover lamb**, and to protect them from the death Angel which was going to pass through the land. Everyone must be dressed ready to leave, the blood had to be applied to the door post and the lintel which is symbolic of our thought life and the works of the flesh. All of the men had to be physical circumcised.

In order to do the **Passover** justice, we would have to look at every spiritual truths, lesson that is wrapped up in the **Passover,** which in itself would easily become a book. Suffice it to say that as we partake of the bread, the grape juice as **Jesus** commanded us, recognizing by faith that it is his body, his blood which he gave for our salvation, faith will begin to rise in our hearts for our deliverance, and Healing. In the Garden of Gethsemane **Jesus** said to the Father: if at all possible let this cup pass from me, but not my will be done, let your will be done. The cup he was speaking about was the cup of cursing. In the old covenant it talks about the curse placed upon sinful flesh. **Jesus Christ** became a curse for us that we might be made free from the curse of the law.[47] **All the congregation of Israel shall keep it.** Everyone that names the name of **Christ** is required to keep the **Passover**. I am not referring to the one that was observed in Exodus, but the one that **Christ** declares today.

John 6:.48 I am that bread of life. 49 Your fathers did eat manna in the wilderness, and are dead. 50 This is the bread which cometh down from heaven, that a man may eat thereof, and not die. 51 I am the living bread which came down from heaven: if any man eat of this bread, he shall live for ever: and the bread that I will give is my flesh, which I will give for the life of the world.... 55 For my flesh is meat indeed, and my blood is drink indeed. 56 He that eateth my flesh, and drinketh my blood, dwelleth in me, and I in him. 57 As the living Father hath sent me, and I live by the Father: so he that eateth me, even he shall live by me.

Back in February 2012 I had an amazing visitation. In a dream I saw the Lamb of God slain. This dream was very precise and intent. Space will not permit me to share it all with you, so let me just share a portion of it.

The Lamb of God! An amazing dream I had!

As I looked into the heavens to my amazement there was the Lamb of God. His wool was glistening white as snow. He was lying upon His side as if He had been slain. His backside was away from me, His underside toward me. Out from His rib, it seemed to be His third rib, from his side flowed a stream of bright shimmering living, quickening blood. Directly in front of His body there had formed a pool of this living blood. I knew there was no bottom to this pool of blood. It is hard to explain what I sensed in my heart as I looked upon His, the Lamb of God's precious living blood. Overwhelming love rose up within my heart for him. His amazing love possessed my heart, my soul, my mind, and my emotions. I was filled with gratitude beyond description for what he **Jesus Christ** the Lamb of God had accomplished for me and others.

As I was looking upon this pool of precious blood, I felt something manifest itself in my right hand. I looked down, and there in my right hand was a branch, a ROD. (This was the specific word that came to my mind) This was not just any ordinary Rod. It was absolutely straight, and it was made of Olive Wood, seemingly seven feet tall. (These are things I just knew to be true in this dream)

Immediately I knew what I was to do with this Rod in my right hand. I lifted this Rod towards the pool of blood in the heavens. To my amazement it seemed to be just the right length to reach up into the heavens. This blood was in the heavens, and yet this seven-foot Rod was able to reach the precious blood of **Jesus**.

I put the end of the Rod right into this pool of living blood. The blood immediately flowed to the end of the Rod. This living blood wrapped itself around the end of the Rod as if it was in absolute oneness with the Rod. Then with my right hand I pulled the Rod back towards me. Once the Rod was back into my Realm (I do not know how else to explain it). I directed the end of the Rod towards my mouth. It looked as if the blood was going to fall off from the end of the Rod, but not a drop fell to the ground.

I opened my mouth wide, and stuck the end of the Rod with the Living Blood into my mouth. I drank all of the blood which had been on the Rod. The very moment that I drank the blood, it was as if an incredible Power exploded inside of me, knocking me flat on my back like a dead man. It slammed me violently to the ground. I cannot properly express how drastic and violent the power of God hit me. **There is power in the blood of the Lamb.**

Revelation 12:11 And they overcame him by the blood of the Lamb, and by the word of their testimony; and they loved not their lives unto the death.

Sense I saw **Jesus Christ** as my lamb over 40 years ago I have never questioned his love for me, or humanity, and yet in order for God to deliver us there are conditions that must be met.

48 And when a stranger shall sojourn with thee, and will keep the Passover to the LORD, let all his males be circumcised, and then let him come near and keep it; and he shall be as one that is born in the land: for no uncircumcised person shall eat thereof.

There must be a circumcision of our heart. *1st Corinthians 11:30* says that many believers are sickly and dying because they are not rightly discerning the Lord's body. They are partaking of the covenant meal by eating the unleavened bread which is symbolic of the flesh of **Christ**, and are drinking the grape juice which is symbolic of the blood of **Jesus Christ,** but they have not been circumcised in the flesh of their hearts.

Romans 2:29 But he is a Jew, which is one inwardly; and circumcision is that of the heart, in the spirit, and not in the letter; whose praise is not of men, but of God.

Now here's some amazing facts about partaking of the **Lamb**. 1st it needed to be cooked in bitter herbs. It was not cooked in honey and brown sugar or with wonderful tasting spices. It was bitter because what **Christ** went through for us was extremely bitter and painful. If they followed exactly what Moses had told them to do, it **would not have been** a very tasteful and enjoyable meal. What **Jesus Christ** went through for us should in our hearts be excruciating and painful, and yet wonderfully beautiful because it is through the **Passover lamb Jesus Christ** we have been made set free.

The **2nd** aspect of the Passover lamb is that all of it had to be devoured. You had no right to pick and choose the best parts. I have ministered in other nations were every part of the animal whether it be a fish, a chicken, or a pig is used. They eat the eyeballs, the brains, the intestines, the feet, every part of the animal is used. We **must eat all of the Lamb** and not just a part of it. *And yes I did eat what was ever put before me.* Preachers who declare that they are called only to preach certain parts of the gospel are deceived. If I only preached what I consider the best parts of the truth, then those who I minister to will not know the whole truth which is designed to set the listeners free from the world, the flesh, and the devil.

Acts 20:20 And how I kept back nothing that was profitable unto you, but have shewed you, and have taught you publicly, and from house to house,

---

Romans 2:28 For he is not a Jew, which is one outwardly; neither is that circumcision, which is outward in the flesh: 29 But he is a Jew, which is one inwardly; and circumcision is that of the heart, in the spirit, and not in the letter; whose praise is not of men, but of God.

The **3rd** aspect is that all the males had to be circumcised. In the New Testament we are required to circumcise the foreskin of our hearts, and we have to circumcise our own flesh. I cannot circumcise your flesh or anyone else's. You must circumcise yourself with the word of God, and obedience to his word. I cannot circumcise the heart of my wife. I cannot circumcise the heart of my sons, my daughters, of the parishioners of the church that I pastor. If you do not circumcise your heart when you eat the **Passover Lamb,** it brings judgment to you. When you eat his flesh, drink his blood it is going to bring faith, or it will bring judgment.

Colossians 2:10 And ye are complete in him, which is the head of all principality and power:11 In whom also ye are circumcised with the circumcision made without hands, in putting off the body of the sins of the flesh by the circumcision of Christ:

God commands us to crucify the flesh by putting to death the deeds, actions, thoughts or attitudes that are against the will of God. The Spirit of faith will rise up, and take authority over your flesh. Without faith you cannot circumcise your flesh. It takes faith to circumcise, to crucify the old man. It does not take any faith for me to attack somebody else and their sinful flesh. It Takes faith to handle people tenderly, gently, softly and meekly. The Scripture says: *in meekness instructing those that oppose themselves if per adventure they will repent to the acknowledging of the truth.*

Remember when the Shepherd boy David faced Goliath the Philistine, he said, who is this uncircumcised Philistine that he should defy the armies of the living God? The whole covenant is based on the foundation of **circumcising your heart. Jesus Christ** overcame the devil as the **Passover lamb**. 26 times it talks about the **Lamb of God** in the book of Revelation.

Revelation 5:12 Saying with a loud voice, Worthy is the Lamb that was slain to receive power, and riches, and wisdom, and strength, and honour, and glory, and blessing.

The **Lamb of God** has defeated the devil, and now God requires us to eat the flesh and drink the blood of the **Lamb of God! Jesus** said **whosoever eaters my flesh and drinks my blood has eternal life**, and I will raise him up at the last day, for my flesh is meat indeed, and my blood is drink indeed. He explains what he means to us in verse 63.

John 6:63 It is the spirit that quickeneth; the flesh profiteth nothing: the words that I speak unto you, they are spirit, and they are life.

You will notice that many ministers today no longer preach **Jesus Christ** and him alone. It is as we meditate, think upon, sing about, read about **Jesus Christ** and who he is, and what he has accomplished, that in a sense we are eating and drinking him. There is no deeper revelation than **Jesus Christ**. He is the glory of the **Father**, manifested in the flesh, seen of men. He said: When you see me you have seen the **Father**. So we are going to eat, drink, sleep, read, think, sing, speak, and meditate upon nothing but **Jesus**.

#8th way that healing comes is by eating and drinking Jesus Christ, and the Word of God!

As we have intimacy with **Christ** we will come into oneness with **Jesus Christ and his word**. Now we can never over emphasize the need to apprehend and the development of our faith in **Christ**. The growing, developing and increasing of our faith is extremely important to our success in receiving the healing that he has made available. Everything that we have, everything that we partake of in **Christ** has to be done by faith. All things were created by God, by faith. God created all things by having faith in himself! Believers are those who do not trust in themselves, but we trust and faith in God.

Psalm 37:5 Commit thy way unto the Lord; trust also in him; and he shall bring it to pass.

Jesus said that at the very end of the ages, right before he came back, would be there any faith left on the earth? The faith that we are talking about is a faith that apprehends the character, the nature, the mind, the heart, and the will of God. A faith that takes a hold of **Jesus Christ,** and brings the believer into a place of victory over sin, the world, the flesh, sickness, disease, infirmities, and the devil. Faith is just like the physical muscles in your body. A lot of people are out of shape physically in America. It is not because we they have any less muscles then other previous generations. We have the exact same muscles that our parents, grandparents, or are great-great-grandparents had. Most people are simply out of shape because they are not exercising their natural muscles. They are not eating the proper type of foods. The natural world is symbolic of what's going on in the spiritual world. People spiritually are not exercising their faith, and they are not eating the proper spiritual foods.

1 Timothy 4:8 For bodily exercise profiteth little: but godliness is profitable unto all things, having promise of the life that now is, and of that which is to come.

People are not exercising physically, or eating properly because for some reason they do not think it is important to do so. This is causing major health problems in our nation. The same thing can be said of our faith spiritually. People are not doing what it takes to develop strong faith in **Christ**. They are also partaking of those things which are very destructive to their faith. Faith in **Jesus Christ** is so vitally important to our Healing, our victory, our success, our overcoming the enemy and everything he throws at us.

We need to see people begin to rise up in faith, and go after the will of God. When faith is in operation it will cause you to pray, gathered together with the Saints, meditate upon Gods word, deny your flesh, share your faith with others, and take care of the needy. We have lost our faith in **Christ** in America, and yet there is still great hope because our faith can be restored in **Christ**. God desires us to have great faith for our Healing, and he has provided for us many different ways to acquire it. All of these blessings, provisions, protections will be activated in our life as we are **dwelling** and **abiding** in **Jesus**.

2 Timothy 1:7 For God hath not given us the spirit of fear; but of power, and of love, and of a sound mind.

There is no fear of what men will do to you, or of sickness, or disease, or poverty, or financial lack, or plagues, or afflictions. There is no fear, there is no worry, and there is no torment when we are walking in the realm of faith, based upon the will, and the word of God. You will have peace that passes all understanding, joy unspeakable, and full of glory. When somebody is sick in the natural we can put our hands on their fore head to see if they are running a fever. The doctor can have you open your mouth, and he will look at your tonsils, or your tongue. Symptoms in your physical body will reveal sickness by certain manifestations. This is also true when it comes to divine faith. If you are truly operating in faith the divine attributes of **Christ** will be manifested. The 9 fruits of the spirit should be evident. You will be living a holy separated, consecrated life for God. If you are not, then it is evidence that you need to step back into that realm of faith by eating and drinking Jesus Christ, and meditating upon God's word.

1 John 5:4 For whatsoever is born of God overcometh the world: and this is the victory that overcometh the world, even our faith.

Psalm 91:1 He that dwelleth in the secret place of the most High shall abide under the shadow of the Almighty.2 I will say of the Lord, He is my refuge and my fortress: my God; in him will I trust.

I mean you're right at home in **Jesus Christ**. You are **living** and **dwelling** in him, you're **abiding** in him. This is a place of such wonderful and deep intimacy. Your fellowship is sweet beyond description. You're not only eating the **Passover lamb**, but you are in fellowship with him. Your mind is constantly stayed upon him.

Isaiah 26:3 Thou wilt keep him in perfect peace, whose mind is stayed on thee: because he trusteth in thee.

Christ has become your **habitation,** your **dwelling** place. You are **dwelling** in **Christ,** and he is **dwelling** in you.

Revelation 3:20 Behold, I stand at the door, and knock: if any man hear my voice, and open the door, I will come in to him, and will sup with him, and he with me.

The table is set before you in the presence of your enemies. God has given his angels charge over you to keep you in all of your ways, and they shall bear you up in their hands lest you should dash your foot against a stone. Now you are able to tread upon the lion and the snake.

Jesus said: behold, I give unto you (they that dwell and abide in **Christ**) power to tread on snakes, scorpions, and over all the power the enemy. **Nothing**, yes he said **nothing** shall be able to harm you. This is such a wonderful place of victorious faith in **Christ Jesus**. I believe this is what Paul declared when he spoke these amazing words in the book of Colossians.

Colossians 3:4 When Christ, who is our life, shall appear, then shall ye also appear with him in glory.

Abiding and **dwelling** is based upon our deep love for God. Notice verse 14 God said because he has set his love upon me, therefore… etc. No one is exactly sure who wrote Psalms 91, but if you look at Psalms 90 it is revealed to us that it was from Moses.

Psalm 90:1 Lord, thou hast been our dwelling place in all generations.

Moses is talking about dwelling in God. In Psalms 91 God says: because you have set your love upon me, therefore will I deliver him, because he has known my name. God is a rewarder of them that diligently seek him. We must believe that God is hearing our prayers. David the Shepherd said: *though I walk through the valley of the shadow of death, I will fear no evil, for thou art with me, thy rod and thy staff they comfort me.* He also declared many are the afflictions of the righteous but the Lord delivers them out of them all.

If you will go through Psalms 91 very slowly, highlighting every time it refers to the person who is **dwelling** and **abiding** in God, you'll discover in 16 versus, this person is mentioned **40** times. It refers to God where God speaks of himself as the Most High, the Almighty, the Lord, refuge and fortress, God - **in him** will I trust over **25** times! Now why would it emphasize **us** more than God? The reason is because God is waiting for us to seek him.

2 Chronicles 16:9 For the eyes of the Lord run to and fro throughout the whole earth, to shew himself strong in the behalf of them whose heart is perfect toward him.

God wants to show himself strong on our behalf, but we must **dwell** and **abide** in him. It is simply amazing to me how the Old Testament saints had such deep understanding and revelation of these truths. They literally saw God as their all and all.

Psalm 27:1 The Lord is my light and my salvation; whom shall I fear? the Lord is the strength of my life; of whom shall I be afraid?

All of the book of Psalms it's very personal and intimate. Many of these Psalms were written by David. He said: I will not fear even if war should rise up against me, in this I will be confident that God will deliver me. David was literally speaking about life and death struggles on the battlefield where he was in jeopardy of losing his life at any moment from sword, spear and arrows, but because he dwelt in God, he had total confidence in his safety and victory.

To me this is amazing faith that can only come by **dwelling** and **abiding** in **Christ**. In the midst of all these battles with dangerous enemies notice what he said: *this one thing I desired of the Lord that I may dwell in the house of the Lord all the days of my life, to behold the beauty of the Lord, and to inquire in his temple*.

Remember when they brought the Ark of the Covenant to Jerusalem, David danced before the Lord with all of his might. King David so desperately wanted to build the temple, and yet God did not allow him to because he had shed so much blood. So his son Solomon built the temple that David wanted to build. Solomon really did not have to do that much when it came to the blueprints or preparations because David had already done it all. David had gathered much of the building materials which were necessary in the construction of this temple. He had gathered much of the wood, the gold, the silver, large stones that were necessary. David had been doing it because it was in his heart to be in the presence of God.

Whenever God's presence is real in your life, you will prosper. So if you are **dwelling**, **abiding** in **Christ**, and his word is **dwelling** and **abiding** you, God will not withhold anything from you.

Psalm 84:11 For the Lord God is a sun and shield: the Lord will give grace and glory: no good thing will he withhold from them that walk uprightly.

Believers need to understand that their faith in **Christ** will never grow until they become aggressive in their fellowship with him. I meet a lot of Christians who are living in the twilight zone. They are out there in the outer limits of entertainment. They are sitting in front of their TV sets, watching soap operas, or there sitting in front of the TV set shouting with Bill O'Reilly: yeah that's right, yeah that's right.

This is the reason why we are not having a move of God. We are not **dwelling** and **abiding** in **Jesus Christ**. It would be almost like you trying to cook your Thanksgiving turkey with the oven set at 150 °, and then shoving the turkey into the oven for only 30 minutes, then pulling it out. There is no way that turkey is going to be cooked all the way through. You might say: Pastor I would never be that stupid, but you know that's exactly what we do when we only come to church Sunday mornings. We are not **abiding** and **dwelling** in **Christ** the way we need to in order to be transformed and changed, to be Healed, and delivered. Faith, Healing will come if we **dwell** and **abide** in **Christ**.

When **Christ** was in his earthly ministry moving in the Holy Ghost, his disciples lived with **him** for 3 and half years. They walked with him, slept at his side, ate when he ate, moved when he moved. They heard him speaking the parables and the teachings that he proclaimed from his heavenly **Father** 24 hours a day, 7 days a week. They saw and experienced everything he did. After the resurrection he appeared to them for another 40 days, continuing to do what he had done before his betrayal, death and resurrection. Why you might ask is this so important? Because he was bringing them into a place of victorious, unwavering confidence and faith in him. According to the Gospels he spent more time with Peter, James and John, because he was cultivating and developing them to be leaders in his church, to be over the other disciples.

Psalm 24: 1 The earth is the Lord's, and the fulness thereof; the world, and they that dwell therein.2 For he hath founded it upon the seas, and established it upon the floods.3 Who shall ascend into the hill of the Lord? or who shall stand in his holy place?4 He that hath clean hands, and a pure heart; who hath not lifted up his soul unto vanity, nor sworn deceitfully.5 He shall receive the blessing from the Lord, and righteousness from the God of his salvation.6 This is the generation of them that seek him, that seek thy face, O Jacob. Selah.7 Lift up your heads, O ye gates; and be ye lift up, ye everlasting doors; and the King of glory shall come in.8 Who is this King of glory? The Lord strong and mighty, the Lord mighty in battle.9 Lift up your heads, O ye gates; even lift them up, ye everlasting doors; and the King of glory shall come in.10 Who is this King of glory? The Lord of hosts, he is the King of glory. Selah.

I want you to notice the King of glory is going to come in and **dwell** and **abide** in us. In verse 3: **who shall ascend into the hill of the Lord, and who shall stand in his holy place?** If you study the word **WHO** it is used in the Bible over **500** times. It's a very interesting study because many times God is talking about **who** it is that will be blessed! In the wisdom books of Job, Psalms, and Proverbs the word **who** is used over **150** times.

3 Who shall ascend into the hill of the Lord? or who shall stand in his holy place? 4 He that hath clean hands, and a pure heart; who hath not lifted up his soul unto vanity, nor sworn deceitfully.5 He shall receive the blessing from the Lord, and righteousness from the God of his salvation.6 This is the generation of them that seek him, that seek thy face, O Jacob.

The Scriptures are very clear and precise about those **who** **dwell** and **abide** in **Christ** will be extremely blessed, healed and delivered.

James 2:5 Hearken, my beloved brethren, Hath not God chosen the poor of this world rich in faith, and heirs of the kingdom which he hath promised to them that love him?

You can **abide** and **dwell** in **Christ** by keeping him at the center of your conversation. For instance I like to go for hikes with my family, and I like looking up into the blue sky, looking at the green trees, being surrounded by nature, all the time my heart and my mind is upon **Christ**, who created, who made all of this amazing world. When you live in this realm, healing and deliverance will flow to you like a mighty River.

CHAPTER NINE

#9 Be A Doer Of God's Word

The **ninth** step, reality truth and receiving your healing is that you must receive, believe, and act upon the word of God. In the gospel of John, chapter 1: verse 12 there is revealed to us a powerful truth.

John 1:12 But as many as received him, to them gave he power to become the sons of God, even to them that believe on his name:

The way the kingdom of God works is completely different than how the natural world works. Spiritual laws, principles, realities are superior than the natural laws that govern nature and humanity. God spoke through the prophet Isaiah in chapter 55 that even as the heavens are higher than the earth, so are God's ways higher than man's ways. As we read the word of God we must simply receive it as it is, and never ever argue with the Bible. Never allow anyone to convince you that Scriptures contradict one another. Never use a Scripture to disprove another Scripture. God has never contradicted himself, and if it appears as if God is contradicting himself, it simply means you're not rightly interpreting the word. God is never wrong, he never lies, he is eternally forever the same, just, holy, and righteous. Once you receive his word, accept it as it is, then verbally you need to say to yourself **"I Believe It"**. The devil will try to convince you that you're smarter than God, which is almost blasphemous in its nature. Always agree with what the word of God says even if it contradicts your experiences, and even the experiences of others.

Titus 1:2 In hope of eternal life, which God, that cannot lie, promised before the world began;

Amos 3:3 Can two walk together, except they be agreed?

Once you verbally declare "**I Believe What God Says**" you are beginning to enter into the realm where all things are possible. Do not be surprised if you have to make this bold statement to yourself over 100 times a day. It will be necessary for you to verbally say to yourself that you believe God's word in order to overcome the spirit of unbelief, which is actually called the spirit of disobedience.

Ephesians 2:2 Wherein in time past ye walked according to the course of this world, according to the prince of the power of the air, the spirit that now worketh in the children of disobedience:

When I gave my heart to Jesus Christ on February 18, at about 3 o'clock in the afternoon, in 1975, I picked up my little green military New Testament Bible, declaring to myself that whatever Bible said, I would believe it. From that time, to this present age I have never argued with the word of God. Yes, I have met many people who have aggressively tried to get me to believe contrary to what Gods word says. They have tried to convince me that there is no hell, but I believe the Bible. They have tried to convince me there is no judgment to those who commit wickedness, and do not repent, but I believe the Bible. They have tried to convince me that healing is not for today, but I believe the Bible. It does not matter how I feel, how it looks, even my own personal experiences. I choose to receive, believe, and act upon the truth of God's word. Jesus boldly declare: **You Have What You!**

Mark 11:23 For verily I say unto you, That whosoever shall say unto this mountain, Be thou removed, and be thou cast into the sea; and shall not doubt in his heart, but shall believe that those things which he saith shall come to pass; he shall have whatsoever he saith.

Saying what it is you desire to come to pass, before you ever experience it, is a spiritual, and biblical truth, whether people like it or not. What you say to yourself will also determine what direction you will go in life. James likens the tongue to the **rudder** of the ship. Though the tongue is very small, even as the **rudder** of a large ship, it can turn about that mighty ship, which is driven by fierce winds.

You are Experiencing What You're Saying, & What You're Saying Is What you are Experiencing!

Do you know that the Scriptures declare that if you're born again that Jesus Christ himself lives inside of you? You might say: I just do not feel like as if Jesus lives in me! When you experience feelings that are contrary to the Bible you have one of two choices. The **first choice** is that you can disagree with God and his word, which in effect is calling God a liar. **Number two** you can say: I believe what God's word says about me, that Jesus Christ lives inside of me, and therefore I agree with God, and I do not care how I feel. How you respond to a situation when you feel something that is contrary to what God's word says will determine the ultimate outcome of your situation. Notice what the diciple of Jesus said in 1John: **You Have Overcome Them Little Children, Because Greater Is He That Is in You Than He That Is in World**! This Scripture is written to all of those who have believed, received, accepted Jesus Christ.

It is a basic principle that if you keep saying something long enough to yourself, eventually you will end up believing it. You can either speak how you feel, the lies of the devil, your circumstances, or you can say **what God says**: to yourself about what God says about you. What you say to yourself continually you will eventually believe, and it will become your reality. This is not mind over matter, but a dynamic spiritual principle, divine laws that God has set in place. Remember When They Were Building the Tower of Babel, and They Were All Saying the Same Thing, and God Made an Amazing Statement:

Genesis 11:6 And the Lord said, Behold, the people is one, and they have all one language; and this they begin to do: and now nothing will be restrained from them, which they have imagined to do.

A major way that I have learned to find out where I am at spiritually is by listening to what I'm saying. When the pressures of life, when afflictions come, when the enemy is attacking me, when I'm under pressure, out of my mouth will come either the truth of God's word, or the lie the devil has fed me. If I find myself saying that which is contrary to God's word it simply reveals that I need to **go back to the Bible**, and put more of the word of God into my heart. It reveals to me that I have not been abiding in Christ, and in his Word the way I should.

God Created Everything by the Words of His Mouth! What you are saying will determine where you will end up living. The place that you are now living in is because of what you have been believing, and confessing over yourself. Please understand that when I talk about confessing God's word I am not talking about you going around and **blabbing** to everybody what you believe. What you say to everybody else should be the tip of the iceberg of what you have been saying to yourself. I spend way more time speaking the word to myself, my mind, my body, my emotions, my circumstances than I do to others.

Ephesians 5:18 And be not drunk with wine, wherein is excess; but be filled with the Spirit;19 Speaking to yourselves in psalms and hymns and spiritual songs, singing and making melody in your heart to the Lord;20 Giving thanks always for all things unto God and the Father in the name of our Lord Jesus Christ;

I married my precious wife back on August 19, of 1978. After being married for a number of years I found myself getting frustrated with my precious wife because she would not submit to me at times. I came up with this (what I thought was being creative) plan in order to get my wife to submit to me. I would simply **Fake** being upset with her, when in all reality I wasn't. So the next time she did not submit to exactly what I asked her to do, I threw a **fake**, miniature hissy fit. I acted like I was mad, and upset with her, acting angry. In all reality I was not angry, but I told her I was, and how I felt about what she did by disobeying me. The next time she did not submit to me, I followed the same routine but with a little bit more emphasis, telling her how upset I was with her. This continued for a number of weeks when all of a sudden to my **horror** I found myself No Longer **Faking** my anger fits, but I was beginning to be totally engulfed with anger and rage at her for not submitting.

Without knowing it I had spoken myself into this satanic attitude. I went to prayer over it asking God what happened? He simply told me that I got what I was confessing. Now, in all sincerity I did not want to be angry and upset with my precious wife. When the Lord revealed this to me, and what I had done, I quickly repented to him, and then I went to my wife, confessing to her what I had been doing, and the results of that manipulation. I repented, asking her to forgive me. Praise God, I was delivered!

Proverbs 18:21 Death and life are in the power of the tongue: and they that love it shall eat the fruit thereof.

---

1 John 5:4 For whatsoever is born of God overcometh the world: and this is the victory that overcometh the world, even our faith. 5 Who is he that overcometh the world, but he that believeth that Jesus is the Son of God?

In the book of Revelation over and over it declares that we must overcome. Those who overcome will be clothed in white raiment, and their names will be written down on white stones that no man knows but God himself. **Jesus** has already overcame all principalities and powers. He said to his disciples in Matthew: *Behold all authority has been given to me in heaven & in earth, go therefore in to the entire world and preach the gospel to every* *creature*. For whatsoever is born of God, overcomes the world! John is very specific about who overcomes. This is John who was the beloved of **Jesus**, the one who laid his head upon the chest of **Jesus** at the last meal. He was the only Apostle who was there at the cross when **Christ** suffered and died. He was the first of the 11 apostles who arrived at the tomb on resurrection morning. John boldly declared that the victory that overcomes the world is **faith** in **Jesus Christ**. Faith is the declaration of trust, reliance, and dependence upon **Christ**. To overcome means to conquer, triumph, prevail, subdue and have victory. Hebrews chapter 11 reveals to us 50 major events that were accomplished by faith in **Jesus Christ**.

What's amazing is that if you look up the word faith in the four Gospels, it appears many times in Matthew, Mark, and Luke, but in the gospel of John the word faith does not appear even one time. Instead we see the emphasis on the word **believe**! Believe and faith are really the same, but the word to **believe** has a deeper and more personal connotation to it than the word faith. It brings to mind a much more intimate relationship.

1 John 5:1 Whosoever believeth that Jesus is the Christ is born of God: and every one that loveth him that begat loveth him also that is begotten of him. 2 By this we know that we love the children of God, when we love God, and keep his commandments. 3 For this is the love of God, that we keep his commandments: and his commandments are not grievous.

In verse three it declares that we keep his commandments. This is a faith that works by love. This is the declaration of our faith in **Jesus Christ**. In one situation **Jesus** asked the multitudes: *why do you call me, Lord, Lord, and do not the things I say?* In another situation, he said: *who is my mother brother and sister, but they that do the will of my Father which is in heaven!*

We are called to keep the commandments of **Christ** and **to do them,** by doing the word of God, you will experience healing! James declares that faith without works is dead. What we do with our time, resources, energy, mind, and body reveals who we really are, because what you love reveals who you are, and that which you love possesses you. **Jesus** declared: *for where your heart is there your treasuries is also*. There is a song I love to sing that declares: *I love to praise him!* There are many Scriptures that declare the love that God's people have for his word.

Jeremiah 15:16 Thy words were found, and I did eat them; and thy word was unto me the joy and rejoicing of mine heart: for I am called by thy name, O Lord God of hosts.

Psalm 119:47 And I will delight myself in thy commandments, which I have loved.

Psalm 119:16 I will delight myself in thy statutes: I will not forget thy word.

Psalm 1:2 But his delight is in the law of the Lord; and in his law doth he meditate day and night.

This is where we come to the **ninth way** in which we receive healing. It is revealed to us from Genesis to Revelation. It is extremely important that we get this deep down into our hearts, this reality of how your healing will come to you.

James 1:22 But be ye doers of the word, and not hearers only, deceiving your own selves.

#9 The ninth way that healing comes is by: **doing whatever the word of God tells us to do!**

Let us read the Scriptures very carefully, taking heed to them.

Romans 2:13 (for not the hearers of the law are just before God, but the doers of the law shall be justified.

James the brother of **Jesus**, who knew **Christ** in a very personal intimate way reveals to us amazing realities of faith.

James 1:23 For if any be a hearer of the word, and not a doer, he is like unto a man beholding his natural face in a glass: 24 for he beholdeth himself, and goeth his way, and straightway forgetteth what manner of man he was. 25 But whoso looketh into the perfect law of liberty, and continueth therein, he being not a forgetful hearer, but a doer of the work, this man shall be blessed in his deed.

Back in 1996 I memorized the book of James word for word because I desired to have these truths within my heart. We must be doers and participators of the word of God. **Faith and healing will come as we act upon the simple principles of the word of God**. In the New Testament alone it talks about doing the word **373** times. When I gave my heart to **Jesus** I determined within my heart that whatever I read in the New Testament that I would do it. Unbeknownst to me I stepped into a major door that God uses to step into our lives. Some of the practical and elemental ways of doing the word of God is as follows. **#1** pray the word **#2** forgive **#3** raise your hands toward heaven **#4** share **Christ** with others **#5** gathered together with believers on a regular basis **#6** give when possible **#7** do good **#8** give thanks **#9** love at all times **#10** never complain **#11** do not speak evil of anyone **#12** cast all of your cares upon the Lord!

In order to do all of these things it will require faith. We need to understand that faith is like a muscle in your physical body, the more you use it the stronger it becomes. Faith is a spiritual muscle, and if you do not work it, then you will lose it!

1Timothy 4:8 For bodily exercise profiteth little: but godliness is profitable unto all things, having promise of the life that now is, and of that which is to come.

James 4:17 Therefore to him that knoweth to do good, and doeth it not, to him it is sin.

2Corinthians 11:3 But I fear, lest by any means, as the serpent beguiled Eve through his subtilty, so your minds should be corrupted from the simplicity that is in Christ.

James also declared that if we do not do the word then we will end forgetting what kind of person we are meant to be. I am not saying that it is easy to do the will of God. We understand when it comes to the development of our physical muscles that in itself it is a challenge. To develop our spiritual muscle called faith will take even more effort than it does to develop your physical muscles, but it is well worth it. Even **Jesus** struggled to stay within the will of the **Father** at times.

Luke 22:44 And being in an agony he prayed more earnestly: and his sweat was as it were great drops of blood falling down to the ground.

Matthew 26:42 He went away again the second time, and prayed, saying, O my Father, if this cup may not pass away from me, except I drink it, thy will be done.

Thank the **Father** that **Jesus** did not fail to obey the will of the Father by Faith. Because of his obedience even to death upon the cross, the **Father** has highly exalted him, and given him a name that is above every name!

James 1:24 for he beholdeth himself, and goeth his way, and straightway forgetteth what manner of man he was. 25 But whoso looketh into the perfect law of liberty, and continueth therein, he being not a forgetful hearer, but a doer of the work, this man shall be blessed in his deed. 26 If any man among you seem to be religious, and bridleth not his tongue, but deceiveth his own heart, this man's religion is vain.

There are many that call themselves believers, but their religion is in vain because they are not exercising any faith when it comes to obeying the word, the will, the plans, and the purposes of God. This is extremely displeasing to our heavenly **Father**. When **Jesus** himself returns with the angelic host he will separate the sheep from the goats. And he will take vengeance on them that have not obeyed the gospel.

2 Thessalonians 1:8 in flaming fire taking vengeance on them that know not God, and that obey not the gospel of our Lord Jesus Christ:

Where Faith Is Alive - The Flesh Will Die!

Jesus declared heaven and earth shall pass away, but my words will never pass away. Every promise, provision, and blessing that **Christ** spoke over his church can be trusted. Now on the other side of the coin I can also guarantee that every warning he spoke will come to pass upon those who will not exercise faith to hear and obey.

Matthew 7:21 Not every one that saith unto me, Lord, Lord, shall enter into the kingdom of heaven; but he that doeth the will of my Father which is in heaven. 22 Many will say to me in that day, Lord, Lord, have we not prophesied in thy name? and in thy name have cast out devils? and in thy name done many wonderful works? 23 And then will I profess unto them, I never knew you: depart from me, ye that work iniquity.

CHAPTER TEN

#10 Remember What God Has Done

The **10th Way, step, principal, truth** in receiving your healing is by remembering what God has done for you, and others. Through the years I have learned to write down whenever I have received answers to my prayers, healings, and miracles. I have also read many books, besides the Bible, of the testimonies of people who have received miracles, answered prayers, and healings. This has greatly increased my capacity to look to God in the midst of being physically attacked by the enemy. Let me share a story with you about the importance of remembering what God has done for you.

I Wrote a 200 Pg. Book in 2 1/2 Weeks (2011)

When God laid it upon my heart to write: Living in the Realm of the Miraculous #1, I had been ministering in a church in Wildwood, New Jersey. In this particular meeting I began to share a number of my amazing experiences that I have had with the Lord since 1975. After the service, pastor Rob told me that people really love to hear the stories. At that moment it was dropped into my heart to go back to the hotel, and begin to write down all of the miracles that God had done in my life. Within two hours the Holy Spirit had brought back to my mind over 120 stories. I simply gave each story a title, with a brief description of the story at that time.

When my wife and I arrived back home in Pennsylvania, the Lord spoke to my heart, leading me to write a book about these experiences. This was so quickened to me by the spirit of God that literally within 2 1/2 weeks I wrote a 200-pg book. (This did not include the editing and the printing of this book). As far as I know, there is no one in my family lineage who has ever even written a book, or even accomplished very much in the natural. My accomplishments are all by the quickening, energizing, power of the Holy Ghost, quickening the word in my heart. God by his spirit has so quickened me, that up to this moment I have memorized 10 books of the New Testament, and thousands of other Scriptures. God is not a respecter of people, and he wants to manifest himself in the supernatural in a powerful way in all of our lives.

There are so many wonderful examples of God's quickening power in the old covenant, for instance when the spirit of God moved upon Samson in an amazing way, Quicken his mortal flesh, causing Samson to do that which in the natural he could never do, by performing incredible feats of strength. Every supernatural divine act of those we read about in the old covenant were performed by the quickening of the Holy Ghost. The spirit of the living God would come upon them, and quickened them to accomplish these feats. Now, we come into the New Testament, based on better and more powerful promises by the redemptive work of Christ. We have a right to partake of the quickening which Christ Jesus himself performs within our hearts and our lives on a moment by moment bases, that's why in Ephesians chapter 3 it makes this powerful statement:

Ephesians 3:20Now unto him that is able to do exceeding abundantly above all that we ask or think, according to the power that worketh in us,

To understand the **10ᵗʰ Way, step, reality, spiritual principle** in which one can be healed we must once again take a look at an example in the old covenant. David is such a central figure when it comes to walking by faith, and being delivered.

Yes, we could use many other historical biblical figures, but what David said and did is such a clear example of how to walk in the supernatural, and how miracles come. Let us take a look at first Samuel 17:

1 Samuel 17:33 And Saul said to David, Thou art not able to go against this Philistine to fight with him: for thou art but a youth, and he a man of war from his youth.34 And David said unto Saul, Thy servant kept his Father's sheep, and there came a <u>lion, and a bear</u>, and took a lamb out of the flock:35 And I went out after him, and smote him, and delivered it out of his mouth: and when he arose against me, I caught him by his beard, and smote him, and slew him.36 Thy servant slew both <u>the lion and the bear</u>: and this uncircumcised Philistine shall be as one of them, seeing he hath defied the armies of the living God.37 David said moreover, The LORD that delivered me out of <u>the paw of the lion, and out of the paw of the bear</u>, he will deliver me out of the hand of this Philistine. And Saul said unto David, Go, and the LORD be with thee.

Now it is obvious that David was a man of faith. And that we must apprehend faith the same way the saints did in the old covenant, even as we must in the new. It is the same faith by which we understand that the worlds were framed by the word of God, and that faith is the substance of things hoped. Faith is literally a spiritual invisible substance just like electricity is a substance, just like nuclear power is a substance. Faith is an invisible force that God used to create and to hold everything together by his word. We need to have this faith by which David used to overcome Goliath. It is by faith that we appropriate the healing which Christ purchased for us by the stripes upon his back.

In Verse 33 King Saul said to David: thou art not able to go against this Philistine to fight with him for thou art but a youth, and he a man of war from his youth. And David said unto Saul:

(now listen to what he says because this declaration is how faith comes)

Thy servant kept his Father's sheep, and there came a lion, and a bear, and took a lamb out of the flock:35 And I went out after him, and smote him, and delivered it out of his mouth: and when he arose against me, I caught him by his beard, and smote him, and slew him. And this uncircumcised Philistine shall be as one of them seeing that he has defied the armies of the living God.

The **10th Way, step, reality, principal** in which healing will come is by reflecting, remembering the victory that God has given to his people, to you and me. Now, some might call this our testimonies, but we're going to take this much deeper. David is remembering what God has done for him, the victories that he has experienced because of his walk with God. You need to know that healing comes when you remember what God has done for you. Did you know that God told Moses to write a book of remembrance?

Exodus 17:14 And the Lord said unto Moses, Write this for a memorial in a book, and rehearse it in the ears of Joshua:

This is how healing will come. Why do you think we have such exquisite details of the life of **Jesus Christ**? The four Gospels are a book of remembrance. We are to remember what God has done for us! Consistently God had the children of Israel to build monuments in order to remember what he had done for them.

Joshua 4:7 Then ye shall answer them, That the waters of Jordan were cut off before the ark of the covenant of the Lord; when it passed over Jordan, the waters of Jordan were cut off: and these stones shall be for a memorial unto the children of Israel forever.

You look up the words remember, remembrance, memorial, Monument, and you will be amazed at how many times God required them to build things, to do certain things, say things, and write certain events down in order that they would remember from generation to generation.

For over 30 years I have lived in Gettysburg Pennsylvania. One thing you'll discover when you get to Gettysburg is that it is a town filled with statues and monuments to the Civil war. This is to remind us Americans of the lives that were lost for the freedom of the slaves, and to keep our nation under one flag. There are many quotes dealing with his particular subject, here is one of them:

"Those who don't know history are doomed to repeat it."
Edmund Burke

Another way for us to remember the past, which is important at times, is to visit a graveyard. The very first items you notice when you enter into a graveyard are the Gravestones! The gravestones are there to remind us of our loved ones. Sometimes when I visit the graveyard where our little girl Naomi was buried (that is her body) I am overwhelmed with emotions that come from the memory of her. Granted there are memories we must subdue and overcome, but then there are other memories we must take a hold of in order for faith to come.

Paul said: *this one thing I do forgetting those things that are behind, and reaching forth unto those things which are before me.* Those things which we must not meditate upon are the things the devil has done, or that we have done against the will of God. Do not allow yourself to be constantly remembering and thinking upon your shortcomings. The enemy will use this to bring defeat into your life. If you have repented in your heart from that which was wrong, then you need to move on. Remember what God has done, and share it with others, then faith will come rushing into your heart as your emotions are overwhelmed with God's goodness and mercy. The Lord spoke to me a number of years ago and he said this: **tell my people that their testimonies are eternal!** I asked the Lord, how is this possible? He spoke to my heart saying: my word is eternal, and it is my word that is at work in them.

Revelation 12:11 and they overcame him by the blood of the Lamb, and by the word of their testimony; and they loved not their lives unto the death.

Have you ever asked yourself why do so many people hate true believers? It is because they remind them that there is a God in heaven! And the day will come when they will stand before him, and give an account of their lives.

The Bible Is a Book of Remembrance!

Why did God give us this Bible? It is in order to cause us to reflect upon who God is, what he has done, and what he has made available to us. If you read the book of Psalms you will discover that David was constantly speaking about calling to remembrance the things that God had done for him.

Psalm 20:7 Some trust in chariots, and some in horses: but we will remember the name of the Lord our God.

Psalm 22:27 All the ends of the world shall remember and turn unto the Lord: and all the kindreds of the nations shall worship before thee.

Psalm 45:17 I will make thy name to be remembered in all generations: therefore shall the people praise thee for ever and ever.

Psalm 63:6 When I remember thee upon my bed, and meditate on thee in the night watches.
Psalm 77:11 I will remember the works of the Lord: surely I will remember thy wonders of old.

Psalm 78:35 And they remembered that God was their rock, and the high God their redeemer.

Psalm 105:5 Remember his marvellous works that he hath done; his wonders, and the judgments of his mouth;

Psalm 119:52 I remembered thy judgments of old, O Lord; and have comforted myself.

Psalm 119:55 I have remembered thy name, O Lord, in the night, and have kept thy law.

Psalm 143:5 I remember the days of old; I meditate on all thy works; I muse on the work of thy hands.

I encourage you to begin to write down every answer to prayer, every miracle, and every time God has been good to you, every time God protected you, and provided for you, and specifically every time that you have received a healing! This has been a routine of mine since I gave my heart to **Christ** in 1975. Every time I begin to reflect and remember all that God has done for me, faith begins to flood my soul. Remember how God has blessed you, because that's what the devil absolutely does not want you to remember. God was constantly encouraging the children of Israel to remember and to remind themselves of all the wonderful marvelous things he had done for them.

1 Chronicles 16:11 Seek the Lord and his strength, seek his face continually.12 Remember his marvellous works that he hath done, his wonders, and the judgments of his mouth;13 O ye seed of Israel his servant, ye children of Jacob, his chosen ones.

If you are having difficulty in trusting God for your healing, simply remember what God has done for you in the past. If you do not have a lot of experiences in God, then simply look at what he has done for others, whether it be in the Bible, or somebody else's personal testimony. Why: you might ask? Because God is not a respecter of people, what he has done for one, he will do for others! If time would permit we could look in the book of Leviticus and we would discover that all of the customs, feast days, Sabbath days, holy days, symbolism, even the construction of the tabernacle in the wilderness was in order for the children of Israel to remember who God is. When God gave Moses the Passover Lamb it was about remembering what God had done for them with a look into the future of the coming of **Christ**. The Scripture even declares in the book of Job that God sends the heavy snow and rain that men may stop and consider him. God designed it for us to stop and remember the one who made all things.

Even the priestly robes were designed with 12 different stones as a reminder of God's will for the children of Israel. Since 1978 I have been wearing a wedding ring to remind me that I have a covenant with my precious wife Kathleen, and when other people see that ring on my finger they know that I have a covenant, and I belong to another.

1Corinthians 11:23   For I have received of the Lord that which also I delivered unto you, That the Lord Jesus the same night in which he was betrayed took bread:24   And when he had given thanks, he brake it, and said, Take, eat: this is my body, which is broken for you: this do in remembrance of me.25   After the same manner also he took the cup, when he had supped, saying, This cup is the new testament in my blood: this do ye, as oft as ye drink it, in remembrance of me.26   For as often as ye eat this bread, and drink this cup, ye do shew the Lord's death till he come.

The apostle Paul emphasized to the Corinthian church that they must call to remembrance what **Christ** had done for them by the partaking of communion. By partaking of communion we are declaring the death and the resurrection of **Jesus**. What **Christ** has done for us is extremely important to our faith, and its development. At every opportunity when I speak at different gatherings I encourage all of the believers to write a book of their **own stories** of what **Christ** has done for **them**.

My wife and I wrote a book called "Living in the Realm of the Miraculous" based upon 127 true experiences that we have had with the Lord. I have written two more since then, and am actually at this moment in the midst of writing the fourth book in this series with approximately 100 more stories. As I read through my own personal experiences, faith begins to rise in my heart, and begins to flood my soul, especially when I'm believing for a healing. I cannot encourage you enough to make **your own book of remembrance** of what God has done for you in all areas of your life. Not only is it important for you to remember what God has done for you, but as others read your stories, including your children and grandchildren, faith will begin to rise in their hearts to believe God.

We need to fully understand that the devil does not like it when we reflect upon, and remember what God has done for us, because that is when faith will come, when miracles will come, when the manifestation of our healing will come. Let us go back once again and look at this particular Scripture about communion. Remember what the unleavened bread symbolizes. It is a declaration of the sinless and holy life that **Jesus Christ** lived when he walked the earth. The bread is symbolic of his physical body which was broken for us. It is speaking about the sacrifice that was paid for our redemption. The bread is broken in half because **Christ** was broke for us, and for our freedom. We are to remember the sufferings that **Jesus** went through for his church, you and I. **Remember the stripes upon his back, 39 lashes for our healing.** Remember the thorns upon his head that declares our freedom from mental, emotional anguish. Remember the holes in his hands and feet, remember all of the abuse, pain and suffering that he bore for our redemption. Remind yourself of the price that **Christ** paid for you to be saved. By partaking of communion I remind myself of the awesome amazing sacrifice that **Jesus** paid.

I can honestly say that from the time I saw by the Scriptures the price that **Christ** paid for me, that I have never doubted his love. He declared at the last supper that the cup of wine was symbolic of his blood. It is this blood that cleanses and redeems us, transforms us, and causes us to overcome the world, the flesh, and the devil. He boldly declared this cup is the New Testament in my blood that is shed for you. As you drink this cup of grape juice do it remembrance of me, **Jesus** said.

As we stand around the communion table, with in our heart and mind we should be saying: **Lord thank you for shedding your blood.** I remember you shedding your blood for my redemption, because without the shedding of your blood there is no remission of sins. Lord I thank you for your blood, and you told me that I am to drink this cup which is a declaration that you have blotted out my sins. I'm supposed to drink it in remembrance, to remind myself of what you have accomplished.

All of the parables were given to us to create within our minds, and hearts images of remembrance. **Jesus** said that the kingdom of God is like a mustard seed planted into the soil, even though is the least of all seeds: but when it is grown, it is the greatest among herbs, and becomes a tree, so that the birds of the air come and lodge in the branches thereof. There are parables dealing with building your house upon a rock, the servants given the pounds, the 10 virgins, and so many more. These are all designed for you to reflect and **remember** in order that faith may rise in your heart, that you may receive the manifestation of your healing. Now when faith arises in your heart it brings peace and joy, life and strength, rest and tranquility. These are all manifestations that faith is at work in a person's heart. Paul declared in the book of

Timothy that God has not given us a spirit of fear, but of power, love and a sound mind.

The kingdom of God is not meet and drink, but righteousness, peace and joy in the Holy Ghost

The Apostle Peter emphasized the importance of calling to remembrance all of what God has done for us. In second Peter he begins to share with the Saints that he is about to depart, and that they must not forget, but call to remembrance all that **Christ** said and did.

3Peter 1:14 Knowing that shortly I must put off this my tabernacle, even as our Lord Jesus Christ hath shewed me.15Moreover I will endeavour that ye may be able after my decease to have these things always in remembrance.16 For we have not followed cunningly devised fables, when we made known unto you the power and coming of our Lord Jesus Christ, but were eyewitnesses of his majesty.17 For he received from God the Father honour and glory, when there came such a voice to him from the excellent glory, This is my beloved Son, in whom I am well pleased.18 And this voice which came from heaven we heard, when we were with him in the holy mount.19 We have also a more sure word of prophecy; whereunto ye do well that ye take heed, as unto a light that shineth in a dark place, until the day dawn, and the day star arise in your hearts:

Remember that **Jesus Christ** is the same yesterday, today and forever! He declares that I am the Lord and I change not! Read the Scriptures and discovered all that God has done for those who have lived before him. Constantly remind yourself of all the wonderful miracles, signs and wonders, healings, and faith will rise up within your heart.

Matthew 4:24 And his fame went throughout they brought unto him all sick people that were divers diseases and torments, and those which we with devils, and those which were lunatick, and the the palsy; and he healed them.

CHAPTER ELEVEN

#11 Speak to The Mountain

Speak to The Mountain, Believing What You Say Will Happen!

The **11th step, principle, reality** that must be apprehended is by speaking to the affliction, sickness, disease, or ailment. Jesus Said in Mark 11: 23

Mark 11:22 And Jesus answering saith unto them, Have faith in God.23 For verily I say unto you, That whosoever shall say unto this mountain, Be thou removed, and be thou cast into the sea; and shall not doubt in his heart, but shall believe that those things which he saith shall come to pass; he shall have whatsoever he saith.24 Therefore I say unto you, What things soever ye desire, when ye pray, believe that ye receive them, and ye shall have them.

The reality is that Jesus already purchased, paid for our healing: physically, mentally, and emotionally when he went to Calvary. In the book of Jeremiah God told the young prophet that he was going to use him to change nations. He gave them a very specific word in chapter 1:

Jeremiah 1:10 See, I have this day set thee over the nations and over the kingdoms, to root out, and to pull down, and to destroy, and to throw down, to build, and to plant.

Notice the job that God had given to Jeremiah was very serious and profound. Now how in the world was Jeremiah going to be able to **root out, pull down, destroy, throw down, build, and plant** amongst these nations? We discover this answer with what God said to Jeremiah.

Jeremiah 1:9 Then the Lord put forth his hand, and touched my mouth. And the Lord said unto me, Behold, I have put my words in thy mouth.

Jeremiah 1:12 Then said the Lord unto me, Thou hast well seen: for I will hasten my word to perform it.

Jeremiah 5:14 Wherefore thus saith the Lord God of hosts, Because ye speak this word, behold, I will make my words in thy mouth fire, and this people wood, and it shall devour them.

Jeremiah 23:29 Is not my word like as a fire? saith the Lord; and like a hammer that breaketh the rock in pieces?

God has given to us his word in order to prevail, overcome, subdue every work of the enemy. We must speak his word to that mountain, problem, adversity that is contrary to God's word and will. We must speak to the cancer, arthritis, disease, and affliction that is attacking our body. Through the years as the enemy has attacked my body, I have had to rise up in faith, taking authority over the affliction and speaking the name of Jesus to the sickness, or disease, and commanding it to go in Jesus name. Christ overcame principalities and powers. He gave unto us authority and power over every work of the enemy. We must take that which has been given to us by Christ, and use it against the enemy.

Luke 10:19 Behold, I give unto you power to tread on serpents and scorpions, and over all the power of the enemy: and nothing shall by any means hurt you.

Abused Woman instantly healed (2010)

I had to go to a local business place and as I was getting ready to go in, there was a precious African-American lady who was moving really slow. She got to the entrance and there was step up. It was only approximately 4 or 6 inches high. She could not even lift her foot that high. I asked her what was wrong and she informed me that her ex-boyfriend and his buddy had beaten her up the night before. She was bruised, black and blue and stiff from head to toe and could barely move any part of her body.

The Lord had been speaking to me about releasing His power through the spoken word. He had Quicken to my heart that I should leave every word that I spoke would come to pass. That Moses and Samuel had come tool the place were not one word they spoke fell to the ground. And that if I would believe the Scriptures, that said we would give an account of every word we speak, and only speak that which you desire to happen according to the will of the father, it would come to pass.

This particular lady turned her back on me as she tried to continue to lift her foot. At that moment, it was quickened in my heart to speak to her body. There was another gentleman standing there waiting to also enter this building. Without even thinking I pointed my finger at her body towards her back and commanded that in the name of Jesus Christ of Nazareth that all of her afflictions, pains and bruising of the beating to be instantly gone in the name of Jesus. I did not shout or speak loud. I simply spoke it at a normal voice. The minute I spoke I perceived that the spirit of God literally hit her body. Instantly, her foot came up real high as if something had been holding it down but now sprang forth being connected to a bungee cords.

She started moving both of her legs and her feet up and down very rapidly. She spun around and stared at me. This may sound strange but she was as white as a sheet (whatever that means). She asked me with a very astonished quivering, mystified and almost in an angry voice, what just happened to me. I preached Jesus Christ and ministered the truth to her. She was still standing there under the power of God as I left. The gentleman who was right behind me stood there watching all of this. I think he was so strong with amazement that he himself could not say anything!

How I Was Healed from Gushing Bright Red Blood!

With what I'm about to share with you, there is no pride, I am not boasting on me, but Jesus Christ. Since 1975 (when I was gloriously born again, and filled with Holy Ghost) every time I get attacked physically by a sickness, disease, or infirmity, I aggressively take a hold of God's promise: **by his stripes I am healed**, and that Christ has given me authority, power, and I can speak to the problem, the illness, or the disease, and commanded to go.

I DO NOT RUN TO THE DOCTORS BECAUSE I DO NOT NEED TO KNOW THEIR PROGNOSIS, MOST LIKELY IT WILL NOT BE GOOD ANYWAYS.

The answer to victory over sickness, disease, and afflictions is not by ignoring them, but by immediately rising up in the name of Jesus, and taking authority over the attack. NOW HERE'S THE STORY!

My wife and I arrived back from Israel on October 30th, 2014. While in Israel I had been experiencing some severe digestive problems. Specifically, when it came to bowel movements. When I got home back to Pennsylvania something was going on inside of me, and it just did not seem right. I sat down on the commode one day and perceiving something was really wrong. As I was having a bowel movement I began to gush bright red blood. When I was finished I stood up, turned around and looked down, and the commode was filled with blood.

Most people would have been immediately filled with fear, called their family members, telling them what was happening, and rushed to the hospital, but this is not how I operate.

PLEASE PAY ATTENTION TO THE STEPS I TOOK TO BE HEALED!

The **1st** thing I did was examine my heart, making sure that there was no sin, or rebellion in my life, and I'm not talking about being sinless. We all have sin, because anything that is not of faith is sin. I am talking about open rebellion, disobedience, bitterness, hate, evil desires, sin in my heart, or life. In order to operate in authority, you must be submitted to the authority of God the Father, Christ, the Holy Ghost, and the Word!

The **2ⁿᵈ** thing I did was that I began to talk to God, thanking the Father for putting all of my sicknesses, diseases, and infirmities upon Jesus Christ, who took it all upon himself including our sins, and our iniquities.

The **3ʳᵈ** thing I did was to **Speak Boldly** to the infirmity in my body, and the demonic powers. and commanding it, and them to go from my body in the Name of Jesus.

The **4ᵗʰ** thing I did was to now **Speak** to my body, my bowels, the intestines, the stomach, commanding them to be healed, and to be made whole. I commanded the blood to stop gushing.

The **5ᵗʰ** thing I did is I began to **rejoice and praise** God that I was healed, not that I was going to be healed!

The **6ᵗʰ** step is that I did not allow myself to be filled with fear, neither did I go around telling everybody, or anybody about the symptoms that were manifesting in my body.

The **7ᵗʰ** thing I did was to continue to thank God from that moment forward that I was HEALED until I saw, felt, and experienced its manifestation! I just kept on thanking God speaking to myself that **I WAS HEALED**.

The **8ᵗʰ** thing I did was to **laugh out loud at the devil**, telling him that he is nothing but a liar, and that God, and his word is true.

How long was it before you saw the manifestation of you healing? To tell you the truth, I do not remember.

Job 5:22 At destruction and famine thou shalt laugh: neither shalt thou be afraid of the beasts of the earth.

Job 8:21 Till he fill thy mouth with laughing, and thy lips with rejoicing.

The **9th** thing I do is that I endure, I stand upon Gods WORD! He that endures to the end will be saved. The word saved in the Greek is the word **SOZO**! This word means: 1), cured (1), ensure salvation (1), to get well (2), made...well (6), made well (5), preserved (1), recover (1), restore (1), save (36), saved (50), saves (1), saving (1). The person who holds onto faith when it comes to divine healing no matter what the circumstance, will be made whole.

The **10th** thing I do is that **I do not** let the symptoms of the sickness, affliction, infirmity control or dictate the course of my life! Now this attack was over a year ago, and I have no more blood in my bowel movements, feeling wonderful, and I am doing good in Jesus Christ.

Not only do I speak to the mountain, but I speak to myself!

Philemon 1:6 That the communication of thy faith may <u>become effectual by the acknowledging of every good thing</u> which is in you in Christ Jesus. 7 For we have great joy and consolation in thy love, because the bowels of the saints are refreshed by thee, brother.

The apostle Paul said that he had heard of their love and faith which they had in the Lord **Jesus Christ**. Then he says something quite amazing by saying that the communication or participation of their faith will become effectual by the acknowledging, sharing or declaring of every good thing which is in us because of **Christ Jesus**. Actually the King James is probably one of the closest correct translations of this particular set of Scriptures. The apostle Paul said by the spirit of God that the **communication of our faith** will cause our faith to grow by the speaking, declaring and acknowledging of every good thing which is in you in **Christ Jesus**. The word acknowledgment means when you admit or declare something that is true and correct! So when somebody says something to you that is obvious, you acknowledge it with a rock solid agreement. So when you agree with what God has said about you, then your faith will begin to increase in your heart. Let me give you some simple biblical examples.

1 John 4:4 Ye are of God, little children, and have overcome them: because greater is he that is in you, than he that is in the world.

1 John 5:4 For whatsoever is born of God overcometh the world: and this is the victory that overcometh the world, even our faith.

Romans 8:31 What shall we then say to these things? If God be for us, who can be against us?

Romans 8:37 Nay, in all these things we are more than conquerors through him that loved us.

Hebrews 13:5 Let your conversation be without covetousness; and be content with such things as ye have: for he hath said, I will never leave thee, nor forsake thee.

Philippians 4:13 I can do all things through Christ which strengtheneth me.

When you begin to agree verbally out loud to yourself with what God has declared about you in his word it will bring healing.

The word communication means to participate, to partake of, and to become one with. What God declares about you and I is absolute truth. Then there are divine truths that God wants you apprehend, but we are not there yet. There are many examples that I could use, but let me use one in particular. Many so-called believers are declaring that they are righteous in **Christ** by faith, but yet they are living like the devil. The minute you believe and surrender to the Lord ship of Christ, God the Father sees you as righteous, but now you must begin to live in it! Many believers have been wrongly taught that righteousness is just a confession when in all actually it must also be apprehended, and worked out by faith in **Christ Jesus**.

2 Corinthians 5:21 For he hath made him to be sin for us, who knew no sin; that we might be made the righteousness of God in him.

Notice the part that says: *that we might be made the righteousness of God in him.* Christ died that we might live in his righteousness.

1 Peter 1:15 But as he which hath called you is holy, so be ye holy in all manner of conversation;16 Because it is written, Be ye holy; for I am holy.

You can declare your holy all you want, but until it is manifested in your heart and your life you are deceiving nobody but yourself. That's where the Scripture would apply in the book of James 1:22

James 1:22 But be ye doers of the word, and not hearers only, deceiving your own selves.23 For if any be a hearer of the word, and not a doer, he is like unto a man beholding his natural face in a glass:24 For he beholdeth himself, and goeth his way, and straightway forgetteth what manner of man he was.25 But whoso looketh into the perfect law of liberty, and continueth therein, he being not a forgetful hearer, but a doer of the work, this man shall be blessed in his deed.

Did you notice in verse 25 it says a *doer of the work*? In Philippians it says that we must work out our own salvation with fear and trembling. Now we know **Christ** lives in us by faith, and people love to make good confessions about themselves which is wonderful, but there is a difference between telling the truth and lying to yourself. You can walk around and declare you're full of the fruit of the spirit all day long when there's no truth to it. What are the nine fruits of the Spirit in Galatians 5? **Love, joy, peace, long-suffering, gentleness, goodness, faith, meekness, and self-control.** You can claim that these are operating in your life when they really are not.

We really need a spirit of discernment when it comes to the declaring what is true in us now, and those things which we still need to work out. For uver 40 years and I've heard a lot of phony baloney, hot air teaching because people are not rightly discerning the word of truth. If you are telling people that you are righteous then they better see the evidence of that righteousness. Yes, the Scripture does declare that we are made righteous through **Jesus Christ,** but it is because of his divine nature and his word at work in us, as we are being doers of the word.

Romans 6:18 Being then made free from sin, ye became the servants of righteousness.

Romans 6:22 But now being made free from sin, and become servants to God, ye have your fruit unto holiness, and the end everlasting life.

Jesus made an amazing statement in the gospel of John.

John 1:12 *But as many as received him, to them gave he power to* **become** *the sons of God, even to them that believe on his name:*

Did you notice **Jesus** said to become, how do we do that? We must do it with the faith that produces action and obedience that we have been ordained to walk in. We really are dealing here with two different issues.

#1 The Acknowledgment of every good thing that is in us by Christ Jesus!

#2 The divine realities which God desires to be manifested and matured in us!

You can proclaim all you want you are full of faith, but that does not make it so. Now we can say God will never leave us nor forsake us, or greater is he that is in me then he that's in the world, or God supplies all of my needs according to his riches in glory, or if God before me who can be against me.

Proclaiming that you're righteous in **Jesus Christ** even when you are committing adultery, stealing, lying being ugly and nasty in your attitude and character is nothing but a lie. That is not faith but it is the spirit of deception at work in you.

The communication of your faith is when you acknowledge every good thing that **Christ** has accomplished for you. I knowledge by his stripes I am healed! I say to myself **by his stripes I am healed.** And I then begin to thank him and praise him for it even though I do not feel it, or see it. Your brain is always working, you're always thinking, most likely muttering to yourself, and what is it that you are thinking and speaking? We need to think and speak that which **Christ** has accomplished for us.

#11 The 11th Way that Healing comes is by the acknowledging of your healing that God has provided for you through Jesus Christ.

Jesus said rejoice because your names are written down in heaven, so Lord I rejoiced that my name is written in heaven. You and I have never seen our name in heaven, but **Jesus** said it so I knowledge it. I acknowledge I am, I have, and can do what God says I am, can do, and have. I boldly declare to **myself: by the stripes of Jesus, I am HEALED**! I know this is true because God can not lie. Here is a wonderful revealing of this truth discovered in the book of Jeremiah.

Jeremiah 1:4 Then the word of the LORD came unto me, saying,5 Before I formed thee in the belly I knew thee; and before thou camest forth out of the womb I sanctified thee, and I ordained thee a prophet unto the nations.6 Then said I, Ah, Lord GOD! behold, I cannot speak: for I am a child.7 But the LORD said unto me, Say not, I am a child: for thou shalt go to all that I shall send thee, and whatsoever I command thee thou shalt speak.8 Be not afraid of their faces: for I am with thee to deliver thee, saith the LORD.9 Then the LORD put forth his hand, and touched my mouth. And the LORD said unto me, Behold, I have put my words in thy mouth.10 See, I have this day set thee over the nations and over the kingdoms, to root out, and to pull down, and to destroy, and to throw down, to build, and to plant.

God had a wonderful plan for Jeremiah. I believe that God has a plan for every person that was ever born, but most do not believe or accept it. *"many are called; few are chosen "*

God said that he would have all men to repent, and to come to the knowledge of the truth, and yet people do not embrace God's plan for their lives! This is the difference between the sheep and goats. Most of what they call Christianity today is nothing but little clicks and clubs were people are just trying to impress one another.

After this experience that Jeremiah had with God his life was never the same. From that moment forward he never argued with what the Lord had spoken to him. Jeremiah said exactly what he had heard God say to him: I am a prophet, and I am sent to the nations in order to warn them of coming judgment. He had to be saying this to himself in order for faith to continue to operate in his life in order to fulfill the difficult task that the Lord had given to him. If you and I are going to fulfill the will of God for our lives we are going to have to begin to talk to ourselves in the same way. You need to declare in the name of **Jesus Christ**: I will love God, I will serve God, I will follow God, and I will go all the way for **Jesus, I am HEALED by the stripes of Jesus**, because greater is he that is in me then he that is in the world.

Another example is when an Angel came to Mary the mother of **Christ** and said blessed art thou among women. God has chosen you to be the mother of the Savior of the world. The Holy Ghost will come upon you, therefore that which you conceive will be of the Holy Spirit, and you will give birth to the son of God, even though you have never known a man. She said let it be done to me even according to your word.

Luke 1:38 And Mary said, Behold the handmaid of the Lord; be it unto me according to thy word. And the angel departed from her.

Faith & Healing will come as you acknowledge, and declare what God has said about you, for you, to yourself.

Whatever you do, do not repeat what fleshly people say about you! They are not the foundation that you build your life upon. Praise God you build your life upon **Jesus Christ** and him alone. We need to saying to ourselves what God says about us, what you're going to do, and where you're going, and act upon it! God says we are healed; therefore, we also declare to ourselves that we are! If we had the time we could talk about many different men of God in the Bible who the Lord told them to call those things which be not, as though they were! For instance, listen to what God said to Abraham in Genesis.

Genesis 17:3   And Abram fell on his face: and God talked with him, saying,: 4 As for me, behold, my covenant is with thee, and thou shalt be a Father of many nations.:5 Neither shall thy name any more be called Abram, but <u>thy name shall be</u>

__Abraham__; for a Father of many nations have I made thee.:6
And I will make thee exceeding fruitful, and I will make nations
of thee, and kings shall come out of thee.

We could take a look at what God told Abraham about Sarah.

Genesis 17:15   And God said unto Abraham, As for Sarai thy
wife, thou shalt not call her name Sarai, but __Sarah shall her__
__name be__.

He has just told Abram to declare that he was Abraham which
means **Father** of many nations. From that moment forward
Abraham began to declare this to himself, and to others. Then God
had Sarai change her name to Sarah, because she was going to be
a mother of many nations. **As far as God was concerned it was
done.** Now Abraham and Sarah had to get it into their hearts. For
faith to come and grow within our hearts, a faith that will
overcome the world, the flesh, and the devil, we must begin to say
what God says about us to ourselves!

IF YOU DO NOT HAVE A FAITH THAT CRUCIFIES YOUR
FLESH THEN YOU DO NOT HAVE A FAITH THAT WILL
SAVE YOUR SOUL!!!!

Victory over Tumors

I woke up one morning with tremendous pain in my lower
abdomen. I lifted up my shirt and looked down where the pain was.
There was a lump on my abdomen about the size of an acorn. I laid
my hands on it immediately, commanding it to go.

I said "You lying devil, by the stripes of Jesus I am healed and
made whole." After I spoke to the lump, the pain became
excruciating and overwhelmingly worse. All that day I walked the

floor crying out to God, and praising him that His Word is real and true. I went for a walk on the mountain right behind the parsonage. It was a long day before I got to sleep that night. When I awoke the next morning the pain was even more severe. It felt like somebody was stabbing me in my gut with a knife. I lifted up my shirt and looked and there was another lump. Now I had two lumps in my lower abdomen. I laid my hands on them, commanding them to go. Tears were rolling down my face, as I spoke the Word. I lifted my hands toward heaven and kept praising God that I was healed. Even though I did not see any change, I kept praising God. All the symptoms were telling me that God's Word is a lie, and that I was not healed by the stripes of Jesus. But I knew that I was healed. It was another long day. It seemed as if I could never get to sleep that night. The pain was continual and non-stop!

When I got up the next morning the pain had intensified even more. Once again I looked at my abdomen and to my shock there was another lump the size of an acorn. Now I had three of these nasty lumps and each were about the size of an acorn. I did not think that the pain could get any worse, but it was. Once again I laid my hands on these tumors, commanding them to go in the name of Jesus Christ of Nazareth. I declared that by the stripes of

Jesus I am healed! It felt like a knife sticking in my gut all that day and night. I lifted my hands, and with tears rolling down my face, kept praising God that I was healed. By faith I began to dance before the Lord a victory dance, praising God that I was healed by the stripes of Jesus. I went to bed that night hurting worse than ever. All night I tossed and turned and moaned, all the while thanking God that I was not going to die but that I was healed. I got up the next morning, and all of the tumors and pain were gone. They have never come back.

CHAPTER TWELVE

#12 Thank & Praise God

The purpose of this book is to help you get healed by faith that is in **Christ Jesus**. Many have realized that they need an education to be successful in the world, so they pay whatever price they need to, and do whatever it takes to get one. Many todays are in desperate need of medical help, and are willing to do whatever it takes in order to get better. There are many other examples I could use pertaining to people giving all they have to possess something they need. The greatest need of all is for us to have faith in **Christ**.

The **12 step, reality, truth** involved in the receiving your healing is that you must Immediately after You Pray, after You Speak to the Mount, after that You Believe That You Receive, you must Begin to Thank, and Praise God. Begin to Thank Him, and Praise Him. Many times after I have prayed, even though it does not seem like I'm really believing that I'm healed, I still begin to praise, thank, and worship God, **Declaring I Am Healed.** Actually in my book on How Faith Comes 28 Ways, I share that praise, thanksgiving, worshipping God is one way that faith comes, grows, and matures. I am talking about having a grateful, praising, and thankful heart. Many times through the years my wife and I have begun to praise God even when it looked like we were not getting any results to our prayers.

Many ministers today are declaring that everything that happens to people is God's fault, or His will. This is one of the most grievous, ridiculous lies propagated by the devil. People teach that God is in control of everything, which is absolutely not the truth. Yes, if God so desired he could stop humanity in its tracks, and he will someday, but at this moment in time He has given us a choice to make. We can choose to follow him, serve him, love him, or disobey him, and ignore him. Based upon these decisions we will reap either life, or death! When people declare that God is in control of everything, it simply reveals their utter ignorance of the workings, the dealings of God. Many bad things take place because we are not submitted, yielded, and obedient to the Lord. It is also because many are ignorant of God's will, or they are not taking the authority which is given to them as believers. The thief comes to steal, kill, and destroy. **Jesus** said: I am come that you might have life, and have it more abundantly. We overcome the world, the flesh and the devil by faith in **Jesus Christ**!

God has given to us amazing tools, weapons, and spiritual truths in order that we might become partakers of his divine nature. His divine nature will only be manifested in us to the degree of our Faith in **Christ Jesus**.

Heb 10:15 By him therefore let us offer the <u>sacrifice</u> of praise to God continually, that is, the fruit of our lips giving thanks to his name.

Notice the word sacrifice in this Scripture. Hebrews is a tremendous book that reveals the sacrifice that **Christ** made for our salvation. Within this book is also revealed that God requires us to continue to sacrifice, not as in the old covenant with the shedding of the blood of animals, but in our life and conduct. It takes faith in order for us to **give thanks and praise to God** when in the natural there seems to be no reason why we should rejoice. I can honestly tell you that this has been one of the **number one ways** that God has allowed me to receive many miracles, and specifically in the area of Healing. As I have rejoiced, praised, thanked and worshiped God in the midst of the hardship, the sickness, the affliction, faith has risen up within my heart for the healing that which God has promised. At the end of this chapter I will share numerous experiences I've had for over 40 years pertaining to this truth.

In the old covenant sacrifices were extremely important beginning with Able, Abraham, Isaac, Jacob, and all the patriarchs of old. This sacrifice of praise and thanksgiving is extremely important in the development of our faith in **Christ Jesus, and in us receiving our Healing**. Let us take a moment and look at some of the definitions for the words revealed to us in Heb 10:15.

Praise: to speak highly of, complement, applaud, standing ovation, salute, or we could simply say YEA to Jesus!

Sacrifices will always cost you something that your flesh will not want to give. When I am in dire circumstances, my emotions and feelings do not want to praise God in the midst of the terrible situation, but if I will simply do this by faith, it brings about a miraculous change in me, which will bring glory to **God** the **Father**. This will be well pleasing to our **Heavenly Father**, causing God to take notice of us. You see faith has a divine fragrance that will attract the attention of heaven. This is not in any way exaggerated, but absolute truth. God is looking for those whose hearts are in agreement (in faith) with him!

2 Chronicles 16:9For the eyes of the Lord run to and fro throughout the whole earth, to shew himself strong in the behalf of them whose heart is perfect toward him.

Hebrews 10:15 also says we are to offer unto God the sacrifice continually! It is not to be spasmodic, temporary, or when we feel like it, but continually offering onto God praise and thanksgiving, especially in the midst of physical affliction. Let us look at this word continually.

Continually: at all times, endlessly, always, evermore, forevermore, perpetually, on a regularly basis!

This word **continually** implies that it must be a daily, moment by moment lifestyle. I cannot emphasize the importance of this act of faith sufficiently. Many are defeated because they will not do the word of God. Faith cannot and will not grow in an atmosphere of disobedience.

Psalm 34:1 I will bless the Lord at all times: his praise shall continually be in my mouth.

Acts 16:25 And at midnight Paul and Silas prayed, and sang praises unto God: and the prisoners heard them.

Ephesians 5:20 Giving thanks always for all things unto God and the Father in the name of our Lord Jesus Christ;

Psalm 145:1 I will extol thee, my God, O king; and I will bless thy name for ever and ever.2 Every day will I bless thee; and I will praise thy name for ever and ever.

1 Thessalonians 5:18 In everything give thanks: for this is the will of God in Christ Jesus concerning you.

Colossians 3:17 And whatsoever ye do in word or deed, do all in the name of the Lord Jesus, giving thanks to God and the Father by him.

Psalm 71:8 Let my mouth be filled with thy praise and with thy honour all the day.

Let us take a look at another set of very important scriptures.

Colossians 2: ⁵For though I be absent in the flesh, yet am I with you in the spirit, joying and beholding your order, and the stedfastness of your faith in Christ.⁶ As ye have therefore received Christ Jesus the Lord, so walk ye in him: ⁷ rooted and built up in him, and stablished in the faith, as ye have been taught, abounding therein with thanksgiving.

Our roots must go deep into **Christ**. He is the vine, and we are the branches. All of our spiritual life flows from **Christ** into us, into every fiber of our being. **Christ** lives in our hearts by faith, this is why it is so important that our faith in **Jesus Christ** must increase on a daily moment by moment basis. Please notice that Paul said that we abound with **Thanksgiving**. This is an amazing revelation that if you will receive this truth, it will transform your life. The definition for abounding means: **overflowing, increasing, multiplication**! There are many Scriptures that confirm this in the New Testament and in the Old Testament.

Psalm 23:5 Thou preparest a table before me in the presence of mine enemies: thou anointest my head with oil; my cup runneth over.

How was David's cup running over? It was by the fact that he constantly was giving thanks to God. Those who are consistently, moment by moment giving thanks to God, no matter what the circumstances they find themselves in, the Scripture declares that they are constantly partaking of a continual feast.

Proverbs 15:15All the days of the afflicted are evil: but he that is of a merry heart hath a continual feast.

Thanksgiving reveals a heart that is filled with appreciation, gratitude, gratefulness which actually is an expression of faith. **Thank you Lord, I just want to thank you**: sang by Andre Crouch is one of my favorite songs. Not only is it faith in action, but it literally will cause you to take off like a rocket in the development of your faith, and receiving your Miracle from God.

Acts 16: 23 And when they had laid many stripes upon them, they cast them into prison, charging the jailor to keep them safely: 24 who, having received such a charge, thrust them into the inner prison, and made their feet fast in the stocks.25 And at midnight Paul and Silas prayed, and sang praises unto God: and the prisoners heard them. 26 And suddenly there was a great earthquake, so that the foundations of the prison were shaken: and immediately all the doors were opened, and every one's bands were loosed.

Not only did Paul and Silas operate in the realm of Faith, but through this experience their **Faith** had a sudden spurt of growth. When we operate in faith God will always supernaturally divinely intervene and show up. Let us look at another Scripture.

Psalm 100:4 Enter into his gates with thanksgiving, and into his courts with praise: be thankful unto him, and bless his name.

We could expand on this Scripture a little bit deeper, even change it slightly to have a correct understanding and interpretation. Let's do that for a moment.

*Psalm 100:4 Enter into his gates (**of faith***) with thanksgiving, and into his courts (**of trust***) with praise: be thankful unto him, and bless his name.*

With the sacrifice of praise and thanksgiving we enter into a new world, the divine spiritual world, the heavenly realm where all things are possible

Psalm 100:3 Know ye that the Lord he is God:it is he that hath made us, and not we ourselves;we are his people, and the sheep of his pasture.4 Enter into his gates with thanksgiving,and into his courts with praise:be thankful unto him, and bless his name.5 For the Lord is good; his mercy is everlasting;and his truth endureth to all generations.

This is why our hearts should be filled with thanksgiving and praise, because the **Lord** is good, yes good, and his mercy is everlasting. Let the sacrifice of thanksgiving flow out of our bellies like rivers of living water. Then there will rise up within us a faith that will overcome the world, the flesh, and the devil. Healing will flow into our bodies like a living river! Miracles cannot but help to flow when our hearts are filled with the atmosphere of praise and thanks giving. The flip side of this coin is that unbelief will grow like a weed when there is grumbling, griping, complaining, faultfinding, and unappreciative thankless hearts! For over 40 years of ministry you would not believe how many people I run into that call themselves Christians who are Grumblers, Gripers, complainers, faultfinders, and just simply negative people. They do not understand why they are living such defeated lives.

Colossians 1: 12 <u>giving thanks</u> unto the Father, which hath made us meet to be partakers of the inheritance of the saints in light: 3:15 And let the peace of God rule in your hearts, to the which also ye are called in one body; and be ye <u>thankful.</u> 16 Let the word of Christ dwell in you richly in all wisdom; teaching and admonishing one another in psalms and hymns and spiritual songs, singing with grace in your hearts to the Lord. 17 And whatsoever ye do in word or deed, do all in the name of the Lord Jesus, <u>giving thanks</u> to God and the Father by him.

The word of God is full of Scriptures commanding us to give thanks, over and over. This is good rich soil in which your faith will grow exceedingly, and become strong and great in **Christ Jesus**.

1 Thessalonians 5:18 In everything give thanks: for this is the will of God in Christ Jesus concerning you.

Ephesians 5:20 Giving thanks always for all things unto God and the Father in the name of our Lord Jesus Christ;

Philippians 4:6 Be careful for nothing; but in everything by prayer and supplication with thanksgiving let your requests be made known unto God.

Psalm 34:1 I will bless the Lord at all times: his praise shall continually be in my mouth.
Psalm 95:2 Let us come before his presence with thanksgiving, and make a joyful noise unto him with psalms.

Psalm 100:2 Serve the Lord with gladness: come before his presence with singing.

I will share with you a number of stories of stories to help you get a good picture of God works!

When I Was Brought Back to Life (1980)

I woke up one morning extremely sick. My whole body ached from my head to my toes, even to the ends of my fingers. It felt as if I had been pulled through a knothole. I cried out to God and came against this satanic sickness. However, I grew worse, and worse all day long. I had an extremely high fever with sweat just pouring off of my body.

Kathee would pray for me throughout the day. I knew I had to shake this thing, whatever it was. So I went outside and began to climb the mountain behind our house. Every thirty feet or so I would get so dizzy that I had to stop and put my hands on my knees with my head bowed to the ground. When this happened I would pray hard. Dizziness and fatigue kept hitting me like the waves of the ocean. After a while I would begin to climb the mountain side again, and it wasn't long before I'd have to stop and bend over again. It felt like I would pass out any second, but I kept on declaring that I would live, and not die.

I think this is where many people make a major mistake: their faith is a passive faith; but biblical, God-given faith is not passive, but it is aggressive and violent. I finally made it up to the top of this small mountain. I remembered where there was a log lying on the ground, so I sat down next to it, and fell unto my back. I just laid there and prayed. When I say I prayed, I mean I kept praising God, thanking God that by the stripes of Jesus Christ I was healed. Eventually, I pushed myself back up, and began to go back down the mountain. When I finally saw the parsonage, I was filled with great relief. I went into the house, feeling worse than ever. I asked Kathee to pray with me. She stayed and prayed at my side. I was burning up with a fever and I needed to get my clothes off. I went to our little bathroom and stripped down to nothing. I was going through terrible flashes. I lay on the linoleum floor hoping to absorb some of its coolness.

Then something frightening happened. I began to sense in a real way that I was going to die. It wasn't exactly fear; it was just something I knew. I cried out to Kathee to come to me. She came into the bathroom and sat down on the floor, putting my head on her lap, praying fervently for me. I could feel my life slowly ebbing out. The next thing I knew my spirit and soul were leaving my body. I was above my wife, looking down upon my body, with my head in her lap. She was crying out to God for me. For a while I simply hovered over the top of myself and my wife. There was no pain or sickness racking me anymore. There was just a total complete peace.

My wife must have noticed that I had died, and she began to commanding me to **LIVE in Jesus Name**! Suddenly, as she was commanding, I felt myself being pulled back rapidly into my body. It was like somebody had turned on a vacuum cleaner and sucked me back into my body. I came to my senses with my head in her lap. It felt like a cold wind was now blowing over my whole body me. I was totally, completely, and instantly healed! The fever and sickness was completely gone. If you ask my opinion of what happened on that day, I literally believe that I died, but my wife's prayers, and her taking authority in Jesus Name brought me back.

Cancer Patient Raised From the Bed of Death

One morning I received a phone call from my good friend, Paul. He told me that he knew of a man who owned a logging company and lumber yard who was about to die. They were waiting for him to expire any day because his body was filled with cancer. Most of it was concentrated in his chest and it had spread throughout the rest of his body. He was located in the McConnellsburg hospital. Paul asked me if I would be willing to go pray for him. I asked him to give me one day to fast and pray for this particular situation. I spent the rest of that day in prayer, fasting, and in the Word.

The next morning Paul came to pick me up. We drove up to the McConnellsburg hospital, praying as we went. We walked into the foyer and up to the information desk. The nurse gave us the necessary information we needed. Paul said he would wait for me and that he would continue in prayer in the hospital's chapel. I found the room where they had put this gentleman, knocked on the door, and entered. They had placed him in a very small room—just big enough to be a closet—that was off the beaten path, like they were just waiting for him to die. He was lying on a hospital bed and was nothing but skin and bones; he looked as if he had just come out of a concentration camp. His skin and the whites of his eyes were yellow. He was a rather tall man who looked to be in his late sixties. He was lying on his bed wide awake. I had no idea what his mental condition was. I began to speak to him and discovered he was totally aware of his surroundings, and actually, I was amazed at how clear and quick his mind was.

I began to speak to him by introducing myself. He almost seemed to take an antagonistic attitude towards me right away. I began to share Jesus with him, but as I was speaking to him, a smirk appeared on his face. He began to tell me stories of the things he had seen in church— supernatural things. He said one time he was in a wild church service where everybody was jumping and shouting. It was quite a number of years ago, and they did not yet have electricity in this church. He said as he was watching people dance and shout, one of them jumped so high that he hit a lighted kerosene lantern, causing it to fall off of the hook. It came crashing down onto the floor and should have immediately broken into pieces and caught the building on fire. Instead, he said it almost acted like a ball. It never broke or went out but landed straight up. The people just kept on dancing and singing to the Lord.

After he told me this story he looked me right in the eyes and said to me, "If I did not get saved back then, what makes you think you are going to get me saved now?" I did not answer him. My heart was filled with deep sorrow and overwhelming love for him. I knew I could not help him, and if was going to get saved and be healed it was going to take God moving upon him supernaturally. I stepped away from his deathbed, and I bowed my head and cried out to God. "Lord, touch this man, help me to reach him because I cannot do it within myself. Lord, You're going to have to touch his heart or he will lose his soul and end up in hell." As I was praying under my breath I sensed the awesome presence of God come flooding into that little hospital room.

Then the Spirit of the Lord rose up within me, and I walked back over to his bed. I began to speak to Elvin once again, but it was under a divine unction of great compassion. I know I did not say very much, but as I was speaking, all of a sudden out of the blue, he began to weep uncontrollably. In just a matter of seconds his heart was completely open to the gospel. He gave his heart to Jesus Christ right then and there. Then I laid my hands on him and commanded his body to be healed. I rebuked the spirit of death, and cancer in the name of Jesus Christ, commanding it to go.

When I was done praying, it seemed to me there was some immediate improvement in his countenance and body. I told him as I got ready to leave that I would visit him again in the hospital. After I left something wonderful happened, but I did not hear the story until later that day when I arrived home from the hospital. Immediately Elvin felt healed in his body. His appetite came back, and the yellow jaundice disappeared completely from his skin and from the white of his eyes. The hospital personnel were amazed at this transformation. They took some new x-rays and discovered that the cancer he had in his body was almost totally gone. The cancer that was in his lungs which had been the size of a baseball was now the size of a cashew nut. In three days' time they released him from the hospital and sent him home. He was working at his sawmill with his son and grandsons within a week!

My Son Healed of an Incurable Affliction

When Daniel was little, he loved to put things in his mouth. While he was in the back seat of my sister's car, he found a can of DW 40. He was always inquisitive and nosey (and still is to this day). When he discovered the can of chemicals, his curiosity and the desire to put things in his mouth got the best of him. He sucked on the end and the cap popped off, so not only did he ingest the DW 40, but it also leaked all over him. By the time we realized what had happen, he was having a hard time breathing. I prayed over him, but he didn't seem to be getting any better. This chemical is not something to mess with!

Kathleen and I got someone to watch Michael while we took Daniel to our doctor right away. Informing the doctor what had happened, he strongly suggested x-rays, so we gave our approval. Lung problems have been a generational curse in my family, and I did not want Daniel to go through the same misery that I and other members of our family had gone through. My mother eventually died from medication related to her lung problems.

When the x-rays came back, the doctor's prognosis was not very encouraging. He showed us the x-rays. The chemicals he had gotten into were very dangerous. The x-ray showed that the chemicals were lining his lungs. Our doctor informed us that there was nothing that anybody could do for him. He also told us that he would always have breathing problems because of these chemicals in his lungs. We thanked him for his help, paid the medical bill, and left his office. From then on it was a fight for his life. Many times late at night I would hear him struggling to breathe. Immediately, I would get up and take him into my arms, and begin to pray over him. I kept commanding the chemicals to come out of his lungs in the name of Jesus Christ of Nazareth. I would keep praying with him in the midst of it thanking, and praising God that he was healed, until he could be breathing normal, and then I would put him back to bed. This went on for many months. I began to notice that after each episode it would happen less and less. It has been over 20 years now since he has had an attack. Thank God, he's completely healed!

CHAPTER THIRTEEN

#13 Laugh at Your Calamity

The **13th step, reality, truth** in you receiving your healing is to **laugh** at the calamities, sicknesses, diseases afflicting your body. Not only should you laugh at the afflictions --- after you have prayed, believed, spoke to the affliction, and have begun to praise the Lord, but then you laugh at the devil also, and all of his lies. Bible Says: we are to **Laugh at our Calamities, Yes, Laugh at Your Enemy!** This is step number **13**. Absolutely, it will take faith for you to laugh at the afflictions, and the enemy, especially when you're full of pain.

There have been many times I have laughed at the afflictions, the attacks of the enemy when there was overwhelming pain and terrible symptoms in my body. Earlier in this book I shared how I had a three-month battle with colon cancer. Many a day I would be walking the floor of the church that I pastor with tears rolling down my face, because of the pain in my body. I would be laughing with what sounded like a very pitiful laugh at the affliction, the symptoms, the terrible pain in my body, and at the enemy. **Why would I be laughing?** When you know someone that is telling you an outrageous lie, what do you do? You laugh at them, at least I do!

Job 5:22 At destruction and famine thou shalt laugh: neither shalt thou be afraid of the beasts of the earth.

Many times through the years (over 40 yrs.) I have laughed in the midst of the affliction, the attacks of the devil. It takes faith to laugh when you're in a midst of an overwhelming attack. Three times I have had all the manifestations that there was cancer in my body. Back in 1980 tumors began to pop up in the lower part of my abdomen. In the late 90s I had all the evidence of prostate cancer. In about 2003 is when the enemy hit me with all the symptoms of colon cancer. In every one of these situations I immediately ran to the **Great Physician whose name is Jesus Christ** of Nazareth. I brought to Christ my situation, and he told me that it was going to be okay because: **By His Stripes I Am Healed! Then I laugh out loud at the devil,** telling the devil that he is nothing but a liar, and let God, and his word be true.

Job 8:21 Till he fill thy mouth with laughing, and thy lips with rejoicing.

Many times through the years Tears have rolled down My Face as I was Laughing at the Devil, and telling him: You're a Liar, a Liar, nothing but a big fat Liar, and I Declare **God's Word Is True,** and My God Cannot, and Will Not Lie!

Hebrews 6:18 That by two immutable things, in which it was impossible for God to lie, we might have a strong consolation, who have fled for refuge to lay hold upon the hope set before us:
In the midst of the physical affliction I have never run for the prayer line, or tried to get a lot of people to pray for me, or with me. You might ask me why not? Is it pride? No, a thousand times no, I just simply know that the affliction is a lie of the devil. The devil is nothing but a liar, and he wants me to doubt God and his word. All of the circumstances, problems, symptoms that are **contrary to the word of God** is nothing but a lie from the devil, and his lying spirit's! I am not saying that we ignore these afflictions because they are lies, but on the contrary, we must aggressively attack them with every weapon that God has given to us.

John 8:44 Ye are of your father the devil, and the lusts of your father ye will do. He was a murderer from the beginning, and abode not in the truth, because there is no truth in him. When he speaketh a lie, he speaketh of his own: for he is a liar, and the father of it.

In the midst of these battles for my life I simply keep telling the enemy that he is a liar, and is nothing but a liar. I boldly declare: **Let God Be True, and every symptom, every pain, every attack of the enemy a Lie!** This is not something I'm telling people, but I am speaking it to myself. At times it may not seem like I really believe it, but as I continue to declare this truth, faith rises up in my heart, and I apprehend that which Christ has purchased for me by his pain, and suffering. The problem with most believers is that they do not see that the enemy has been defeated. Sickness, and disease, afflictions have been defeated by the stripes of Jesus, but we must take it by faith.

Psalm 2:4 He that sitteth in the heavens shall laugh: the Lord shall have them in derision.

This may sound ridiculous, but through the years I have dared the devil to try to kill me. Now, some would say: **oh you better not do that!** You better not challenge the devil! **Why not?** David spoke boldly to Goliath. Saints of old were not afraid of their enemies.

Proverbs 28:1 The wicked flee when no man pursueth: but the righteous are bold as a lion. Deuteronomy 28:7 The Lord shall cause thine enemies that rise up against thee to be smitten before thy face: they shall come out against thee one way, and flee before thee seven ways.

Isaiah 26:3 Thou wilt keep him in perfect peace, whose mind is stayed on thee: because he trusteth in thee.

Psalm 112:7 He shall not be afraid of evil tidings: his heart is fixed, trusting in the Lord.

Psalm 27:1 The Lord is my light and my salvation; whom shall I fear? the Lord is the strength of my life; of whom shall I be

afraid?2 When the wicked, even mine enemies and my foes, came upon me to eat up my flesh, they stumbled and fell.

This is not pride, but I am boasting on God. My boast is in the Lord and I will rejoice in God my Savior. I literally tell the devil and the demonic world! **You Cannot Kill Me**, I am a child of God, I am washed in the blood of Jesus, I am more than a conqueror through Jesus Christ who loved me and gave himself for me. I am the blood redeemed, and I am seated in heavenly places in Jesus Christ. Devil, I double dog dare you to try to kill me. Now to many Christians this would seem absolutely foolish, prideful, and arrogant, but to me:

I'm poking the devil in the eye with the divine stick of the cross of Calvary.

At the same time that the enemy is attacking me, in the middle of this battle, deep within my inner man I have a Merry heart. My heart is merry because I know I cannot be defeated. If God before me, then who can be against me? God is given to me so many wonderful powerful promises which if I will believe, they will cause me to laugh at calamity, at the affliction, at the enemy of my soul.

Proverbs 15:13 A merry heart maketh a cheerful countenance: but by sorrow of the heart the spirit is broken.

Proverbs 15:15 All the days of the afflicted are evil: but he that is of a merry heart hath a continual feast.

Proverbs 17:22 A merry heart doeth good like a medicine: but a broken spirit drieth the bones.

Let me ask you a question: have you ever ran in to a habitual liar? Once you discovered the person that you are speaking to is nothing but an **absolute liar**, how do you respond to him? If he said something to you that was threatening, or slanderous, or accusative, how did you respond? My natural response is that **I laugh at them**! I say: oh yeah, right.

When I was growing up I had a cousin who I knew very well. He was a **notorious exaggerator** that would inflate the smallest truth into an overwhelming mountain. Everybody in my town knew that he was an exaggerator. The last time I saw him was about 10 years ago. I visited him on a farm where he was renting a house. He told me that he was now a major deer breeder. He did have a couple of deer there on the premises. I think he told me that he had 30 other farms.

I asked my brother Billy, who still lived in that same town if there was any true to him having 30 deer breeding farms? He laughed, and told me "**oh that's just Rodney**", and you know how Rodney is! To this day if you are in that little town, and if you say something that seems completely exaggerated, they will still say: **Oh Yeah, right Rodney**! His name has become an expression of exaggeration. If this is true about this man, how much truer is it about the devil. **Whose report will you believe?** God who cannot lie, or the devil who cannot tell you the truth.

Psalm 52:5 God shall likewise destroy thee forever, he shall take thee away, and pluck thee out of thy dwelling place, and root thee out of the land of the living. Selah.6 The righteous also shall see, and fear, and shall laugh at him:

Now You Understand I'm Not Living in Sin, I am not Out of the Will of God, and I'm Not giving Place to the Devil. Once you realize that the attack of the enemy is nothing but a complete an absolute lie, you will begin to laugh at him. You will not waste your money, or your time on the medical world. You will take a hold of God, speak his word, thank him in advance that it is done, and laugh at the enemy.

Terrible Warts Gone Over Night

A poverty-stricken couple began to come to our church. We watched as Jesus set this couple free from drugs, alcohol, violence, and immorality. We helped install a new bathroom in their little house. The wife became one of the main workers in the church. She was always there trying to help people.

One day they brought one of their young daughters to us. They told us she had a problem they did not know how to resolve. They had taken her to the doctor, but there didn't seem to be anything they could do. The girl was hiding behind them so her mother brought her to the front. Then she had the girl hold out her little hand. It was terrible. Her little hand was completely covered with warts front and back. We are not talking about twenty or thirty warts. It literally looked like hundreds of warts. We laid our hands on her little hand. We then commanded these foul warts to come off of her hand in the name of Jesus Christ of Nazareth, and for her hand to be completely healed.

As we looked at her hand, it did not seem as if anything happened. We told them that when you pray in faith, you must believe that those things you asked for in faith are done. We explained that what we need to do is begin to thank God that she is healed—that the warts are gone in the name of Jesus. Both the husband and the wife agreed that it was done. They took their little girl, got in their car, and left.

The next morning, I received a phone call from the mother. She was extremely excited and bursting with happiness. She told us that when her little girl went to bed that night nothing had changed. The warts were just as bad as ever. When she went to get her the next morning, every single wart was gone but one. They brought the little girl back to us to look at her hand. Sure enough, in one-night God had removed every single wart but one, which was in the palm of her hand! The skin on her hand was smooth and normal just like the other one, as smooth as baby skin. We declared that the last remaining wart would have to leave also!

Dangerous Attack of Conjunctivitis! (1993)

I am sharing this story in order to help you to understand how to take a hold of your healing. You see John 10:10 says that the thief comes to steal, kill and destroy. It tells us in the book of James to submit ourselves to God, resist the devil, and he will flee from us. The very minute that any type of physical affliction attack our bodies is the very moment that we need to take a hold of God, and then come against the enemy of our souls. *Our bodies are the temples of the Holy Ghost, and the enemy has no right to afflict them.*

One of the brothers of the church where I pastor went with me to the Philippines. We were ministering in the province of Samar, which is one of the five provinces of the Philippines. It takes an airplane ride from Manila, and then transferring to ground vehicles. The trip is rather long, tiring and challenging. Not including the fact that we are in the territory of the New People's Army, which is an anti-government communist movement. Believe me when I tell you that they will kill you in a heartbeat.

When we finally arrived at our destination, the Filipinos we were working with were waiting for us. The local pastors and believers had already prepared the way for us to hold crusades in different towns and villages. In the natural they really did not need us because they are all walking in the realities of God. To some extent we Americans are like White Elephants in that we draw a crowd. We do not have any more of the Holy Spirit or the word of God than they do.

As we were on our way for the first set of meetings all of our team including myself was attacked with Conjunctivitis, commonly called Pinkeye. Conjunctivitis is caused by a virus that can be dangerous in two ways. First, the person with the infection can lose some of their vision; in severe cases they can totally lose their eyesight. This could be for a short time, or it could be permanent. Second, the infection can spread very rapidly, and is highly infectious. People with "pink eye" often get conjunctivitis germs on their hands by rubbing their eyes, then leave the germs on the objects they touch.

The first sign of this affliction is that your eyes begin to feel dry and irritated. And then it gets to the point where it literally feels like someone has grabbed a handful of sand and shoved it into your eyes, grinding your eyeballs slowly with the sand. The whites of your eyes eventually turn pink, and can become blood red when it's really bad.

The very minute my eyes began to become irritated, I found a quiet place of prayer. I simply spoke to my heavenly Father thanking Him for what Jesus had done for me when He had received the stripes upon his back. After meditating upon these realities for a while, it was time to take my authority that Christ has given to all believers. I spoke the name of Jesus to this affliction, commanding it to go, now, now, now in the name of Jesus Christ of Nazareth. No ifs, ands or buts! And then I followed through with thanksgiving, praising and thanking God that I was healed. Not that I was going to be healed, but that I was healed, now! From that moment forward it did not matter how I felt, or looked. I knew that I knew that I knew that I was healed. I just kept thanking God and praising God quietly, and in my heart.

I went on my way rejoicing even though it did not feel any different, or look any different. Not one more word came out of my mouth to anyone about this affliction, or how terrible my eyes felt. Within less than two days all of the symptoms were gone.

I'm sorry to say that this was not the case for the rest of the team. A lot of these precious people were going through terrible irritation. The brother I had brought with me began to get much worse. Eventually the white of his eyes turned blood red. I knew in my heart that if we did not do something he could go blind.

This continued for over a week, when he finally came to me telling me that he had to get back to America. I have learned a long time ago to not be critical of people, but to work with them where they are at. He told me that I could continue the meetings, but he was leaving. I informed them that I would go with him making sure he was going to get back home. He was my responsibility as his pastor and also the spiritual authority of these meetings.

Of course my precious Filipino brothers were slightly upset because there were meetings that still needed to be fulfilled. I informed them that I was sorry but my first responsibility was to this brother, and that the Holy Ghost would move through them, and speak through them.

In order to cut our trip short, it was going to take faith to get on the plane earlier than when we were scheduled to leave. And we also had to believe that we were not going to be stopped by customs because of the highly contagious affliction in his eyes. All the way home he kept dark sunglasses on. Through a series of miracles, we were able to board a plane early and get back to America.

The infection that he had picked up in the Philippines did not leave him without medical help. Thank God he did not lose his eyes. Jesus always worked with us where we are at. My position is one of being there for people no matter what. We help, pray and encourage where we can. If we do not see a miracle we simply keep our eyes on Jesus. If we fall short, we just determine in our heart to get back up and keep on going. If I run into situations where it does not seem like I can receive healing, I just go deeper into God, his word, and his will for my life. *God will never let you down!*

Arthritis Could Not Stay! (Generational curse)1996

There are generational curses that are passed on from one generation to another. These are satanic strongholds that must be broken. In my family lineage there were quite a number of these strongholds. My personal family members and I have, and had, numerous physical infirmities.

When I gave my heart to Jesus Christ, and began to intensely study the word of God, I discovered that I was free from the curse of the law. I began to aggressively take what Christ had purchased for me with the stripes on His back. By faith I began to cast down these physical strongholds. Not only did I receive healing for my own personal body, but I also declared that in the name of Jesus these physical afflictions would not be passed on any longer. My sons and daughters and their children would not have these afflictions.

One of these afflictions that were passed on from generation to generation is arthritis. My sister Deborah began to experience arthritis in her late 20s. At one time she had been a very gifted typist and piano player, but before she was in her 40s, her fingers had become gnarled and almost unusable. Arthritis had entered her body so dramatically that I remember her crying with pain and great suffering.

By my late 20s and early 30s arthritis began to try to manifest itself in the joints of my fingers. The minute that pain came to my hands I began to speak to them even as Jesus declared in the gospel of Mark 11:23 and 24. I submitted myself to God, resisted the devil by speaking to the affliction and commanding it to go. And then I began to praise God, and thank God that by faith I was healed In the Name of Jesus. No matter how my hands or fingers felt I thank God that I was healed.

Sure enough after a day or two the stiffening and pain would completely dissipate from my joints. Through the years it has tried to come back, but I have not allowed it. I know this may sound braggadocios, but it's not. This is a reality that Christ has given to every believer.

CHAPTER FOURTEEN

#14 You Have Need of Patience

The **14th step, truth, reality** in your healing is **Patience!** It is very difficult for many people to patiently wait for the manifestation of their healing. One of the major problems is that they associate their healing with the manifestation. For another words they do not believe that they are healed until they feel it, see it, and experience it. Patience is directly connected to our faith and that which we are hoping, believing for. In Hebrews 10:38 emphasizes the importance of enduring and having patience.

Hebrews 10:36 For ye have need of patience, that, after ye have done the will of God, ye might receive the promise.

Having patience is like a long-distance runner. In high school I used to run cross-country track. A sprinter and a long-distance runner is two different things. A sprinter may run 100 yards, whereas a long-distance runner will have to run many miles. Speed is necessary for a sprinter to win a race. Cross country runners not only need speed, but they need endurance. In the thesaurus the **Synonyms** for endurance are:

abidance, ceaselessness, continuance, continuity, continuousness, durability, duration, continuation, persistence, subsistence

There are many scriptures in the Bible that deals with the subject of patience and endurance when it comes to the believer and his faith. As we are believing God that **We Are Healed,** we will have need of patience and endurance.

Matthew 24:13 But he that shall endure unto the end, the same shall be saved.

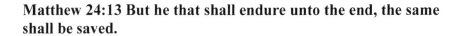

Mark 4:17 And have no root in themselves, and so endure but for a time: afterward, when affliction or persecution ariseth for the word's sake, immediately they are offended.

1 Corinthians 13:7 Beareth all things, believeth all things, hopeth all things, endureth all things.

2 Timothy 2:3 Thou therefore endure hardness, as a good soldier of Jesus Christ.

2 Timothy 4:5 But watch thou in all things, endure afflictions, do the work of an evangelist, make full proof of thy ministry.

Hebrews 6:15 And so, after he had patiently endured, he obtained the promise.

In the book of James the brother of Jesus gives to us wonderful insights on the importance of patience. Many believers have the wrong concept in thinking that the minute they prayed that if they are in faith they should have an immediate manifestation of their healing. The Bible says that they that believe shall lay their hands on the sick, and **they shall recover**. Please notice the word **recover**. It implies a length of time involved in the manifestation, or the evidence of the healing. Yes, I love it when I pray for someone, or myself, and see instantaneous results. If I do not see instantaneous results this does not mean that I am not healed, or the person I prayed for is not healed. The Scripture says that **they shall recover**.

Many times when I pray for people I will encourage them to go ahead and check to see if there is any change in their body whatsoever. Most times there will be a little bit of a change in their physical condition. When Peter prayed for the man at the gate beautiful, the Bible says he received strength in his ankle bones.

Acts 3:5 And he gave heed unto them, expecting to receive something of them.6 Then Peter said, Silver and gold have I none; but such as I have give I thee: In the name of Jesus Christ of Nazareth rise up and walk.7 And he took him by the right hand, and lifted him up: and immediately his feet and ankle bones received strength.

It was after Peter prayed that this crippled man received a little bit of strength in his ankle bones. This man **immediately acted upon that little bit of a manifestation** and he began to leap, and dance. He acted upon that little bit of a manifestation in his body without being told to! His actions were a manifestation of his faith.

Many times when I have prayed for people with bad backs immediately after I pray I tell them to reach for their toes with their fingertips. At their first stretch most of them can barely bend over. I tell them to reach once again with their fingers for their toes. The second time they can go about half way. I tell them once again to reach further for their toes with their fingertips. By the third time that they stretch for their toes, acting upon my instructions, many of them see the manifestation of their healing. We must act upon that which we have spoken by faith over our bodies. If you do not see instantaneous results, you must never let go of the fact that by his stripes **You Were Healed!**

James 1:3 Knowing this, that the trying of your faith worketh patience'

James 1:4 But let patience have her perfect work, that ye may be perfect and entire, wanting nothing.

James 5:10 Take, my brethren, the prophets, who have spoken in the name of the Lord, for an example of suffering affliction, and of patience.:11 Behold, we count them happy which

endure. Ye have heard of the patience of Job, and have seen the end of the Lord; that the Lord is very pitiful, and of tender mercy.

When I Take a Hold of the Will of God, specifically when it comes to my Healing, I am Speaking the Word, I'm Thanking God, I'm Laughing at the Devil, and during This Time of Patience I keep an attitude of FAITH! **I Am Thanking God That His Word Is Real, and I'm Laughing at the Devil**. It is like starting a fire in your fireplace. Once you have a flame burning in the wood stove, you keep feeding the fire fuel until it is a raging, hot, enduring flame. If you are using a wood fire in your house to keep your house warm you must naturally be putting wood in the fire all through the day, and through the long cold night in order that the fire will not go out. It is the same with receiving your healing. You must maintain a constant faith by acting upon the word until you see the manifestation.

Romans 8:24 For we are saved by hope: but hope that is seen is not hope: for what a man seeth, why doth he yet hope for? :25 But if we hope for that we see not, then do we with patience wait for it.

Many times after I have received my healing the day will come when the enemy will attack me in my body exactly in the same area where I have already received the victory. Once again I'll take a hold of the word of God, standing upon the truth, and go through the whole process again. Healing always comes to me as I act upon the truth.

Let Me Go over These **14 Points** once again very quickly. **Number 1-** You must enter into the Arena of Faith. **Number 2-** You Must Be Extremely Serious about your healing. **Number 3 -** Never Exalt the devil or the Afflictions. **Number 4 -**You Must Exalt Jesus Christ above all else. **Number 5 -** recognize that Jesus Paid the Ultimate Price. That He Took Your Sicknesses and Diseases. **Number 6 -** God Absolutely Wants You to Be Healed. Don't Listen to any Lie that the devils Tell You Otherwise. **Number 7 -** Examine Your Heart and Simply Confess Your Sins.

Repent and Turn Away from Them, Believing God to Get Victory over them. Do not Think for a moment that You Have to Be Sinless before You receive the manifestation of your Healing. **Number 8** - Eat and Drink the Word of God Night and Day. **Number 9** - Believe and Do the Word of God. **Number 10** - Remember and Write down the Miracles you have experienced. **Number 11** - Speak to the Mountain, Believing What You Say will come to pass. **Number 12** - Immediately Begin to Thank and Praise God that you are healed. **Number 13** - Laugh at Your Calamity. Laugh at the devil. Laugh at the Symptoms. Laugh at the Problems no matter how long they continue. **Number 14** - You Have Need of Patience That after You Have Done the Will of God You May Receive the Promise!

My Busted broken bruised finger Healed!

We all do stupid things; that is just a part of our humanity. The question is: Will God still heal us in spite of our stupidity? I have discovered many times that the answer to this question is yes! Here is another example of something stupid I did and God was still there for me.

One day I walked into my son Daniel's house. He was in his front room playing a videogame. It's something called PlayStation Move, where he was playing a game called Sports Champion. He held a wand in his hand, thrusting it and waving it back and forth aggressively. As he was doing this, there was another man on the big screen TV following his moves as a fighting opponent. Right then and there I should have turned around and walked out, but curiosity got the better of me. He asked me if I wanted to play a game with him because you could have two players at one time fighting each other. I thought about it for a while and decided, yes I would play. So he handed me another wand, showing me how to activate it. The object of the game was to wave and thrust the sword on the video by waving the wand in my hand. The man on the screen would follow my movements and fight for me.

He started the game console and we began. Of course, I had never played this game before nor do I make a habit of playing video games, so he was winning. I began to get more aggressive trying to win the game but no matter how much I tried, my son seem to be able to score points against me. I totally gave into my flesh and began to wave, stab and wave my make-believe sword everywhere. I mean I really aggressively got into this thing. In the process of trying with everything inside me to win this game I did not notice that I had gotten close to hitting a heavy duty metal case that he had in his front room. Before I knew what I did, I was sweeping the sword to the right down away from me with all my might, and slammed my right hand into the corner of this metal cabinet. I am telling you that I really slammed my hand extremely hard. My son Daniel said I hit the cabinet so hard that it put a dent in the cabinet. The minute I hit that cabinet with all my might, pain exploded through my body. I looked at my index finger and it was all mangled and twisted. Immediately, it swelled up turning black and blue and was twisted. Just looking at my busted up index finger made me sick.

I began to jump around holding my finger with my other hand. And this is what I was crying out to God as I was jumping and screaming, "Lord, please forgive me for being so stupid. Lord, I will never play this game again. I'm so sorry, Father God, in the name of Jesus I repent. I kept jumping around holding onto my finger crying out to God saying: I repent, I repent, I repent. Forgive me, Lord!"

My son Daniel looked at the finger and said dad you broke it, you are going to have to go to the doctor. With my finger so full of pain and my other hand holding it, I told him I did not need a doctor that I had Jesus Christ and he is the great physician. After I made sure that I had sufficient repentance, I spoke to my finger. I commanded my bones to be knit back together and for my finger to be made completely whole. And then I began to thank God that I was healed. I just kept praising the Lord that my finger was made whole no matter how it felt or how it looked.

The spirit of God must have spoken through me at that moment because I told my three sons that by tomorrow morning my finger would be completely well and you would not be able to tell that I had ever slammed it by being so stupid. When I was finished making this declaration of faith, I walked away from them holding onto my finger. Even though the pain was throbbing through my body, I just kept thanking God that I was healed.

My son Daniel still remembers very vividly how busted, twisted, broken, black and blue my finger was. I believe that he thinks it was rather funny how I was jumping around confessing and repenting and promising God to never do this again. I went to bed that night and fell asleep holding onto my finger, thanking God that I was healed. I was meditating on the Word and confessing that what Jesus did for me when he had taken the stripes on his back had the ability to completely make me whole from stupid accidents that were my fault.

The next morning when I woke up early to pray and seek God, I had completely forgotten about my finger. And then it hit me that there was no pain. I looked at my index finger and you could not even tell that I had busted, broken and bruised it. I was completely healed! I went and showed my three sons what God had done for me in spite of my own stupidity. God is so awesome and amazing. All we have to do is cry out to Him and He will answer and deliver us from every situation if we simply trust, repent and obey him; giving praise and thanks no matter how it looks. How long do we keep thanking and praising God? We are to keep on knocking and to keep on asking until we receive the full manifestation of that which we believe for!

Matthew 21:14, And the blind and the lame came to him in the temple; and he healed them.

How I Received Healing for a Busted Kneecap! 1989

We had very heavy snowfall this particular winter. I owned an old John Dear snowmobile that I had made available to the local fire department if they ever needed my help. Eventually, they called me up during a terrible winter storm telling me that they had a heavy equipment operator that needed to be transported to Orrtanna.

He first needed to be picked up at his house and then delivered about 6 miles away. I informed them I would be more than willing to do this for them, especially because I love adventures. Actually, I am a snow addict. I can never get enough snow. The snowstorm and sleet had not yet abated and was raging in all its fury. I told my wife Kathleen that the fire department had called with a job for me to do. Mike to the rescue, or so I thought. I dressed up in all my winter trappings. I then went out and brushed the snow off my John Dear snowmobile and laid my hands on it, commanding it not to give me any problems. I should have prayed over myself first. I started the old machine up, revving the throttle as I headed out of the church parking lot. I turned to my right going down the deserted, main highway. There I was, having the time of my life and doing it for the fire department! Here I was doing about 50 miles an hour or faster, when I hit a section that was nothing but black ice.

The snowmobile's back end spun to the right out of control. I went flying through the air as it threw me for a lopper. I slammed my right kneecap extremely hard on the asphalt road. I felt my kneecap rip, break and tear as I kept sliding down the road for quite a distance. The snowmobile had continued on its way, spinning out of control. The snowmobile itself eventually stopped because my hand was no longer cranking the throttle. Fortunately, it was not damaged because there was nothing but snow in every direction. There I was, lying on the road in the snow and freezing wind, clutching my busted up knee, alone and in tremendous pain! Immediately, I cried out to Jesus and repented for being so stupid and for not using Godly wisdom.

My theology is that almost everything that goes wrong in my life is usually my own stupid fault. Even if the devil is involved in it, it is most likely because I first opened the door for him. After I was done repenting and confessing to the Lord, I went aggressively after my healing. I commanded my kneecap to be put back into its normal condition in the name of Jesus Christ of Nazareth. I commanded every broken part of it to be made whole. You see, I could grab my patella and move it all around. It was no longer attached to my knee. It seemed to have become completely disconnected, no longer restrained by its associated ligaments.

Probably at this juncture, most people would have called it quits when it comes to completing the mission they set out on. But that is not my mode of operation. If I declared that I was healed then I needed to act upon it. I discovered a truth a long time ago, God cannot lie! So, I slowly crawled back over to my snow machine and pulled myself back into the seat. I painfully swung my right leg over the seat into its proper position. At that very moment, wave after wave of pain overwhelmed me. Years of experience walking in faith, however, caused me to declare that I am healed in the name of Jesus. In the name of Jesus, I am healed. I opened the throttle and proceeded on the way to pick up the equipment operator. I kept proclaiming the truth.

On the way, there were a lot of areas where my snowmobile just would not go. The snow was way too deep in some areas to go or the road was flooded with water in others. The storm had dumped a combination of rain, ice and snow. One would need a boat to go through some of the areas where I went. Admittedly, at times I took chances that I should not have taken. I would accelerate to a high speed and just zip across the flooded areas. The back end of the snowmobile would begin to sink as if I wasn't going to make it. But, I would constantly revert back to the old trusted declaration: In the name of Jesus, in the name of Jesus, in the name of Jesus, I will make it. There are a lot of wonderful messages preached on faith but that's not what wins the victory. It is when the Word has been quickened in your heart that you know, that you know, that you know, that you know that God and His Word are true.

I cannot describe to you enough the immense pain and agony that I was going through, yet I did not merely think that I was healed, I knew that I was healed! Faith is not thinking, hoping, or wishing. It is knowing that you know, that you know, that you know. I finally reached my first destination. The township worker saw me pull up outside of his house. As he came to the machine, he could not see my face because of my helmet and my ski mask. I did not tell him that I had an accident and possibly shattered my kneecap. I do not adhere to bragging about the devil or his shenanigans, lies or deceptions. This was no little man that I had to carry on the back of my machine either. He mounted up and we were on our way. It took major faith to keep on going. We had to take numerous detours before I finally got him to the big earthmover that he was tasked to operate. He jumped off my snowmobile and thanked me for the ride. I told him it was no problem as I opened up the throttle and headed home.

This time, I decided to take a different route because the last route was so bad. It took all the faith that I could muster to get back to the parsonage. I was cold, wet, tired and completely overwhelmed with pain from the shattered knee. When I got home, I just kept thanking God that I was healed. During the next couple of days, I refused to pamper my leg. I did not put any ice or heat upon it. I did not take any kind of medication or painkillers. I did not call anyone asking them to please pray for me and to believe God for my healing. I know this may seem extremely stupid, but I knew in my heart that I was healed. It has got to be in your heart! My head, my body and my throbbing, busted kneecap were all telling me that I was not healed, but let God's Word be true and every symptom a lie. When the next Sunday rolled around, the roads were clear enough for people to make it to church.

During that time, you might have called me Hop-Along Cassidy because of the way that I was walking. I do not deny the problem, but I sure as heaven denied the right for it to exist! One of our parishioners, who was a nurse, saw me limping badly. She asked me what happened and I told her. She informed me that this was a major problem. She tried to explain to me in medical terms exactly what she thought I had done to my knee. Medically, in order to reattach and repair my patella, I would have to endure at least one major surgical procedure. She recounted to me that she had once had a similar injury although it was nowhere near as bad as mine. She went on to elaborate that even after an extensive operation, her knee was still giving her major problems. I thanked her for this information and went back to trusting and believing that by the stripes of Jesus Christ, I was healed.

I sure as heaven was not going to let go or to give up on God's promises. I wrestled with this situation day after day, commanding my knee to be healed and to function as God had designed it to do. When the pain would overwhelm me, I would tell it to shut up, be quiet and work! When it seemed like my leg would not carry me, I would command it to be strong in the name of Jesus. This went on for well over a month. One morning I crawled out of bed and my knee cap was perfectly healed. You would think that when the healing manifested that I would begin to sing, shout and dance, but I did not and I do not! You see I had already done all of my rejoicing in advance because I believe that the minute I prayed, I received!!!

IMPORTANT INFORMATION: YOUR PREPARATION TO RECEIVE HEALING BEFORE YOU ARE PRAYED FOR & HANDS ARE LAID ON YOU! THIS WILL GREATLY INCREASE YOUR OPPORTUNITY TO BE HEALED!

#1 1st realize and boldly confess, God wants to heal me more than I want to be healed. It is God's will to heal me, no matter what I have done. It gives God great pleasure to heal people because he is a God of love and compassion.

#2 Go through the 4 Gospels looking for every time Jesus healed people. Notice the Scriptures declare he healed them all. Every single person Jesus prayed for was healed. Most instantaneous, some progressive as they went, but they were healed.

#3 Recognize that Jesus was the perfect will of the father manifested in the flesh. That everything Jesus did was based upon the fact that the father told him to do it. Hebrews says that Jesus Christ is the same yesterday today and forever. If he ever did it once, he will do it again.

#4 Get It Out Of Your Head, that you do not deserve to be healed. None of us deserve to be healed, it is God's mercy, love and kindness. Get it out of your head that the sickness you have is Paul's thorn in the flesh, or God trying to teach you something. These are all lies from the devil. Jesus Christ, God the Father, and the Holy Ghost are all eager and desiring to make you whole.

#5 Try to prepare your heart with great faith and expectation for what God is going to do through the whole day if possible. Get ready because God will not only heal that one particular problem you have, but he will be doing many other wonderful things for you in when you prayed for.

#6 Began to boldly declared to yourself (and others if you want to) that when hands are laid on me, Jesus Christ himself will touch my sick disease body and I WILL BE MADE WHOLE! NO IFS, ANDS OR BUTS! I WILL BE MADE WHOLE! TODAY IS MY DAY TO BE HEALED, TO BE DELIVERED, TO BE SET FREE.

#7 BEGIN TO PRAISE GOD RIGHT NOW, THIS VERY MOMENT FOR YOUR HEALING, FOR YOUR DELIVERANCE, FOR YOUR FREEDOM! I AM EXCITED ABOUT WHAT WE'RE GOING TO SEE GOD DO IN YOU, TO YOU, AND EVEN THROUGH YOU!
Sincerely: Dr Michael H Yeager

ABOUT THE AUTHOR

Dr. Michael and Kathleen Yeager have served as pastors/apostles, missionaries, evangelists, broadcasters and authors for over four decades. They flow in the gifts of the Holy Spirit, teaching the Word of God with wonderful signs and miracles following in confirmation of God's Word. In 1983, they began Jesus is Lord Ministries International, Biglerville, PA 17307.

Websites Connected to Doc Yeager

www.docyeager.com

www.jilmi.org

www.wbntv.org

Books Written by Doc Yeager:

"Living in the Realm of the Miraculous #1"

"I need God Cause I'm Stupid"

"The Miracles of Smith Wigglesworth"

"How Faith Comes 28 WAYS"

"Horrors of Hell, Splendors of Heaven"

"The Coming Great Awakening"

"Sinners In The Hands of an Angry GOD", (modernized)

"Brain Parasite Epidemic"

"My JOURNEY To HELL" - illustrated for teenagers

"Divine Revelation Of Jesus Christ"

"My Daily Meditations"

"Holy Bible of JESUS CHRIST"

"War In The Heavenlies - (Chronicles of Micah)"

"Living in the Realm of the Miraculous #2"

"My Legal Rights To Witness"

"Why We (MUST) Gather!- 30 Biblical Reasons"

"My Incredible, Supernatural, Divine Experiences"

"Living in the Realm of the Miraculous #3"

"How GOD Leads & Guides! - 20 Ways"

"Weapons Of Our Warfare"

Made in the USA
Middletown, DE
02 April 2016